STUDYING FILMS

ALSO AVAILABLE IN THIS SERIES

FORTHCOMING

STUDYING EALING STUDIOS

Stephanie Muir

Dedication
In memory of John, who lived with me in Ealing. Also for our grandchildren Jordan, Lulu, Abi and Billy, in the hope that they will grow to love the films.

First published in 2010 by
Auteur, The Old Surgery, 9 Pulford Road, Leighton Buzzard LU7 1AB
www.auteur.co.uk
Copyright © Auteur 2010

Series design: Nikki Hamlett
Cover image: detail from *Passport to Pimlico* poster © Aquarius Collection
All DVD framegrabs taken from the respective Region 2 DVDs of the Ealing Studios films discussed, distributed by Optimum Classic Releasing / Studio Canal
Set by AMP Ltd, Dunstable, Bedfordshire
Printed and bound in Poland; produced by Polskabook

British Library Cataloguing-in-Publication Data
A catalogue record for this book is available from the British Library

ISBN 978-1-906733-31-5

Contents

1. EALING AND BRITISH NATIONAL CINEMA

Ealing Studios: An 'Icon of England'[1]

Ealing Studios, located in the West London suburb from which it takes its name, is one of the best loved and best known of all British cinema institutions. Many of the 96 films made at Ealing between 1938 and 1955 under its head of production Michael Balcon appear as examples in studies of British national cinema. It has become a brand name representing a particular kind of institutional practice, a community of film-makers working together in a defined location, producing a particular kind of film. Within the context of a nation having to adjust to a devastating conflict, the consequences of its aftermath and the social upheavals that followed, Ealing films can be considered as reflecting some common characteristics which can be identified as 'national', conjuring up images of Britain and Britishness for a home as well as an international audience. In many ways the values of Ealing in the 1940s and the early 1950s have become identified with the values of Britain. Seen from its own particular perspective – described by John Ellis as 'liberal rather than radical, progressive rather than revolutionary'[2] – it can be studied as constructing an image of an entire nation at a particular moment in its history.

British National Cinema: Some Meaning beyond Geography?

British cinema comprises the whole vertical industry: the emphasis is economic. British cinema has as much to do with how films are produced, distributed and exhibited as with the process of film-making itself. ... Out of British cinema emerge British films. This seems like a truism; but if by British films something indigenous is meant, then it is not. Balcon's activity [at Ealing] in his half-century as film-maker and celebrant of Britain may be seen as, first, establishing a continuity for British film-making and, later, giving the idea of a national cinema some meaning beyond geography. **Laurence Kardish** [3]

When discussing British national cinema we can begin by using the description formulated by Jeffrey Richards as 'the population that collectively occupies a defined territory'.[4] The word 'collective' here suggests one nation, a territory the inhabitants share and thus contribute to a common ideology that shapes their values, character and national identity. In Britain the notion is complicated by the fact that we are a United Kingdom where 'England' has often stood for 'Britain' and the separate parts of Wales, Scotland and Northern Ireland have their own distinct identities. In the past few years, however, debates around national cinema have shifted their emphasis. Not only has the concept of a homogenous British identity been revised in the light of multiculturalism and devolution but also the definition of what constitutes a British film is also subject to debate. Today the production of films is dominated by finance which often crosses national borders, coming from outside Britain in the shape of Hollywood or European co-productions. The dominance of Hollywood both financially and culturally has always been regarded as a challenge to indigenous cinemas but in the 21st century new technologies and conglomerates have positioned cultural products as transnational and audiences as global. Spectators now have the ability to access world cinema, not as elitist screenings in selected specialist cinemas or non-populist TV channels but in digital accessible forms. However the films themselves are often marketed as distinctive examples of particular traditions, enjoyed by much of their audience for their difference to the recognised Hollywood model.

In this respect the films made at Ealing in the 1940s and early 1950s can be examined for this distinctiveness; their depiction and use of what we might see as key signifiers of Britishness; their pleasures often deriving from their deviation from the Hollywood film. We might say that in this particular period what could be labelled 'British' films might be divided into four categories:

- **British films.** Made in Britain, usually set in Britain, with British finance, using British writers, directors, actors, creative and technical personnel: *Brief Encounter* (dir. David Lean, 1945 Cineguild), *The Wicked Lady* (dir. Leslie Arliss, 1945 Gainsborough Pictures).

- **British 'international' films.** Made in Britain with an aim to rival the high production values of Hollywood, often with 'international' themes, nearly all British personnel: *The Thief of Bagdad* (dir. Ludwig Berger/ Michael Powell, 1940 London Film Productions), *Anna Karenina* (dir. Julian Duvivier, 1948 London Film Productions).

- **British 'transatlantic' films.** Made in Britain with American finance by the British arm of a Hollywood studio. British technicians, some American actors, creative personnel and values, ensuring appeal to American audiences: *The Citadel* (dir. King Vidor, 1938 Metro-Goldwyn-Meyer British Studios), *Goodbye Mr Chips* (dir. Sam Wood, 1939 Metro-Goldwyn-Meyer British Studios).

- **'Hollywood British' films.** Made in Hollywood from British plays, novels or history, set in Britain. American personnel: *The Private Lives of Elizabeth and Essex* (dir. Michael Curtiz, 1939 Warner Brothers), *Mrs Miniver* (dir. William Wyler, 1942 Loews/ Metro-Goldwyn-Meyer).

The films made at Ealing Studios belong to the first category, which still allows for the inclusion of creative personnel who were not originally British or British citizens – such as composer Georges Auric and producer Monja Danishewsky – but whose contributions undoubtedly added to the overall British 'feel' of the films.

British Values: Projection and Reflection

> *It would be easy to slip into saying that...given Ealing's intentions, the films can be taken to reflect and project some kid of universal truth about the England of the time: a truth which is there and which they express... Even the recording faculty of the camera may capture only superficial aspects of the period... however, the concept of projection and reflection can still be useful. The films at least project their maker's picture of Britain and the British character.* **Charles Barr** [5]

When studying Ealing Studios as a unified product it is useful to return to the older concepts of national cinema. The time and place in which the films are so deeply rooted and the industry that they so richly represent can be looked at as important components in the construction of our national, cultural and social identity. Charles Barr's definitive book *Ealing Studios* grew out of an article he wrote for *Screen* in 1974 entitled 'Projecting Britain and the British Character'. Michael Balcon, in an interview he gave in 1969, stated his philosophy:

> *I think we all came here convinced that films made in this country should be from the roots right down into the soil – should be absolutely indigenous... that sounds dramatic but I don't intend it to be, but I do happen to think that the only nationalism that's worth a damn is cultural nationalism when films are absolutely rooted in the soil of this country.*[6]

In any attempt to comprehend what an identity is, it is useful to look at what it is not. This ties in with discussion of a national cinema as one that is very different to that of Hollywood while at the same time disregarding the notion that Hollywood is the norm from which all others derive or deviate. Ealing Studios may be the nearest the British film industry ever came to one that mirrored the classic Hollywood example but the films that emerged from the Studio were very different to their American counterpart. The 'Britishness' of the Studio can be examined in several ways:

- The **context** of production – both the wider (historical, social, political, cultural) and the industrial (available technology, finance).

- The **organisation** of production that determined what kinds of film would be made and created the environment that would shape them.

- The **ideology** of the creative group making the films and their understanding of the values and beliefs of their audience.

In an article written in 1931 Michael Balcon defined what he considered made a film essentially British. This included 'native simplicity and sincerity', 'making pictures which express England', 'a suitable standard of English' and a 'national style' which he was later to suggest to have been established by the British Documentary movement.[7] These concepts can be located within the struggle for British film-makers to establish their own national cinema. Britain, a nation with a relatively small population, was Hollywood's most profitable market. The USA had a large home audience and producers who could recoup their initial investments domestically and sell their escapist productions cheaply abroad. The introduction of the talkies in 1927 only served to further intensify the differences between Great Britain and the USA. It underlined the fact that the two nations may share a common language but this language with its different accents and modes of speech expressed dissimilar social and ideological attitudes. America was an emerging power whose culture was defined by enterprise and energy rather than tradition.

These perceived differences in American and British outlook were exacerbated by the presence of the Allied American Forces on British soil from 1941. Films such as *The Way to the Stars* (dir. Anthony Asquith, 1945 Two Cities) stressed these differences. The Americans on the Air Force base are loud and ostentatious, their flamboyant behavior contrasting with the emotional self-control of the British characters. The film highlights the British virtues of getting on with it, not making a fuss and hiding your feelings.

Restraint as a British characteristic informed many of the so-called 'quality' films produced during British cinema's most successful period in the 1940s. The War had provided the impetus for a national cinema focused on the ideas and values of a nation under threat. Critics heaped praise on British films for their perceived realism and restraint in contrast to the fantasy and sentiment of Hollywood. Most of the film directors were middle class, some public school educated with a stiff upper lip tradition. The schism between quality and popular cinema is encapsulated in two films both released in November 1945 – *Brief Encounter* and *The Wicked Lady*. *Brief Encounter* is the quintessential film about British denial and control, with longing sacrificed to decency, and passion sublimated and channelled into art making it culturally respectable. Quotations from Keats, music by Rachmaninov and images of surging trains underline the loss which must have been experienced by many women (and men) after six years of war and the realisation that life was now returning to the humdrum and the everyday. *The Wicked Lady*, derided by critics but popular with audiences, indulged in a feast of excess overtly displayed in the torrid affair between Barbara and the highwayman Captain Jackson and the flamboyant *mise en scène*. However it also in a sense sublimates the passion it arouses by channelling its audience's longings for excitement away from the here and now and into the past, where the Romantic novel and the bawdy Restoration romp were the more flamboyant expressions of British identity. Between these two examples of national cinema sit the films made at Ealing Studios, their commitment to realism exhibiting a different kind of middlebrow low-key Britishness as a little island holding out against the vast surrounding ocean of American culture.

1   Ealing Studios listed on the '*Icons of England*' website www.icons.org between 'Pay and Display' and 'Eccles Cake'.

2   John Ellis (1975) 'Made in Ealing', in *Screen* (16)1: 105.

3   Laurence Kardish (1984) 'Michael Balcon and the Idea of a National Cinema', in Brown and Kardish, *Michael Balcon: the Pursuit of British Cinema*, New York: The Museum of Modern Art, p. 43.

4   Jeffrey Richards (1997) *Films and British National Identity: From Dickens to Dads' Army*, Manchester: Manchester University Press, p. 1.

5   Charles Barr (1977) *Ealing Studios*, New York: The Overlook Press, p. 8.

6   Balcon interviewed in 1969, in *Omnibus*, 'Made in Ealing. The Story of Ealing Studios', dir Roland Keating, BBC broadcast, 2 May 1986.

7   'Sincerity Will Make the Film English', *The Era* (London), 11 November 1931, p.10 as quoted in Kardish, *op. cit.*, p. 45.

2. MOVING PICTURES AT EALING

Cinema began in Britain in January 1896, a month after the first public screening of a moving image by the Lumière Brothers in Paris. *Rough Sea at Dover*, by British film-makers Birt Acres and Robert W. Paul, played to the Royal Photographic Society in London. This began a highly productive period with early British films being as inventive as their opposite numbers in France and the United States. Amongst those whose interest in photography led them to become pioneers of British cinema was Will Barker.

Barker founded the Autoscope Company in 1901 and in 1902 the Will Barker Film Company bought West Lodge and The Lodge, two houses on Ealing Green in grounds of nearly four acres backing onto Walpole Park. The adjacent row of well-proportioned houses led to Pitzhanger Manor, once owned and rebuilt by the architect John Soane, lending the whole ensemble an air of elegance. In front was the 'village' green with its mature horse chestnut trees and in the nearby streets the development of chic Edwardian villas provided the genteel, suburban and middle class setting that earned Ealing the nickname 'Queen of the Suburbs'. Barker began producing films there, building a studio with tall glass walls and a glass roof, echoing the one Méliès had constructed in 1897 in Montreuil-sous-Bois, Paris. By 1912 Ealing was one of the largest film studios in Europe, releasing many silent productions under the name of Bulldog Films.

Other film studios were established around London (such as Twickenham in 1913, Borehamwood in 1914 and Lime Grove in 1915) helping to provide some of the British films that comprised 25% of films shown in British cinemas. However in spite of their early promise these films began to lag behind both those of Europe and the USA. American film companies established bases in Britain, and even before World War I their competition posed a threat to both British and European film production as British audiences began to get a taste for the more polished American films. After the 1914–18 War the USA moved in to close the gap left by the difficulties of British film production during wartime. British films failed to respond to the changing market or make up the lost ground. There were problems in funding an industry often looked on as mere entertainment and thus inferior to the perceived intellectual demands of the theatre. By the mid 1920s the industry that had begun so positively was struggling, even 'facing oblivion'.[8] By 1926 only 5 per cent of all films shown in British cinemas were of British origin. The importance of having a national industry was recognised by the Government and the Cinematograph Films Act of 1927 attempted to redress the balance by establishing a quota. The Act demanded that a percentage of British films were distributed and exhibited and restricted the practice of 'block booking' American films into cinemas. This had several consequences. It boosted British film production, drawing new talent into the industry even if the results were the much derided 'quota quickies', and led to Hollywood Studios beginning to make major investments in the British film industry in order to circumnavigate the Quota.

The protection given by the Act was surely a factor in the decision of London theatre producer Basil Dean to begin to raise the finance to build the first purpose built sound stage in Britain on the Ealing site in 1928, the year after the first sound film was released by a Hollywood studio. He found a backer in Stephen Courtauld, a member of the wealthy Courtauld textile family, who would continue to provide finance for the studio until 1952. By 1933 two sound stages were completed and the company was renamed Associated Talking Pictures (ATP). Between 1931 and 1938 about sixty films were made at Ealing by ATP and other producers who rented out the studio space.

British Cinema during the 1930s

Dean took over Ealing as the industry moved from silent to sound films and by 1932 the British share of the market had risen to 24%, boosted by the demands of providing films to fill the new theatres being built in Britain's cities. The creation of cinema chains, often housed in magnificent Art Deco structures, was the work of perceptive investors such as Oscar Deutsch. As Jonathan Glancey has noted:

> The sheer energy of Oscar Deutsch, creator of the Odeon cinema chain, remains breathtaking. In just 10 years between the founding of the chain and Deutsch's death in 1941, 258 Odeons opened throughout Britain, more than half of them in new buildings. They brought not only the latest British films and Hollywood movies, but also a standard of contemporary design that was absent from the lives of most people in these determinedly old-fashioned islands.

> With their cloud-piercing towers and sweeping lines, Odeons were a promise of the shapes of things to come. For less than a shilling (five pence), coal miners, railway workers, teachers, nurses, servicemen, typists and clerks could disappear into a shining world of futuristic dreams, a whole dimension away from the grim economic and political reality.[9]

A regular stream of films was needed to fill these theatres. By the mid 1930s eight of the twenty most popular films were British made. They were often drawing audiences at home but Dean experienced difficulties in distributing ATP films through RKO into the American market. Coming to film production from the theatre, however, he understood the rapport that existed between the performer and the audience, exemplified in the traditions of the British Music Hall. His coup at Ealing was to offset the more serious productions with popular ones and bring to the studio two established stars from the North. Gracie Fields from Rochdale and George Formby from Wigan both had huge box office appeal. They offered British audiences what has been described as an 'attainable ordinariness' with their broad Lancashire accents, direct approach and positive working class Britishness. Their films contained songs that became cemented into popular culture, drawing in the spectators that Glancey identifies who took the opportunity to engage with one of their own. 'Our Gracie' became a symbol that could represent a wide spectrum of identities, with an all embracing personality that was, as Jeffrey Richards puts it: 'simultaneously Rochdale, Lancashire, Britain, the Empire, women and people at large'.[10]

Sing as We Go (dir. Basil Dean, 1934 ATP), Gracie's fourth film at Ealing, was written by the Yorkshire playwright J. B. Priestley. Set in the mill towns of the industrial north and the seaside resort of Blackpool it begins with the closing of the mill. A film about unemployment (at the time of its release nearly two and a half million British people were on the dole) it is also about spirit and resilience. Gracie loves and loses but exhibits the kind of hardiness that was to become a feature of the representation of women during the conflict only five years away. The stoicism of 'Don't worry, I'll be alright', 'there's now't to cry about, now't to cry about at all', leads to ultimate victory, in this case the reopening of the cotton mills.

George Formby became Britain's top male box office star and the highest paid entertainer in the British Isles. In contrast to the suave, assertive Hollywood male leads such as Clark Gable and Ronald Colman George was a moon faced, accident-prone innocent. The secret of his appeal lay partly in this apparent innocence for behind that façade of gormlessness George was the master of innuendo who could be rude whilst appearing to be a prude, although his risqué lyrics were subject to censorship by the BBC[11] who held the monopoly on broadcasting. He made his first film at Ealing in 1935, *No Limit* (dir. Monty Banks, ATP), and ten more there between 1935 and 1941.

By 1936, however, the British film industry was in the middle of yet another crisis. Several studios closed down. The Government responded by revising the Quota System in 1938, setting a 'minimum cost test' and giving Hollywood studios even more incentives to put money into British films. The importance of the British market to American producers encouraged their colonisation of the British film industry and American production companies were able to capitalise on gaps in the legislation. MGM set up studios at Borehamwood. The films made by Hollywood companies were 'transatlantic', ensuring their appeal to American audiences by featuring American stars (and American values) but using British technicians. MGM-British's head of production was Michael Balcon.

Sir Michael Balcon[12]

Michael Balcon, one of the most fervent champions of British cinema, was a Jewish second generation immigrant from Birmingham. His patriotism was founded on his love and 'faith in the country which in the last century had provided sanctuary for [his] forebears'.[13] His daughter Jill described this in 1986 as:

*People whose parents have been refugees feel an
enormous love for the country that's given them roots.
Sometimes people who are not entirely British can see in a
more detached way, as well as in an affectionate way, what
we are like.*[14]

Balcon's unfaltering and undoubted patriotism was summed
up by director and cinematographer Ronald Neame who
described him as:

*Staunchly British – so British that in some ways he
damaged Ealing whilst at the same time enhancing its
reputation tremendously because I think there was a
time that he even put a Union Jack on the end of the
film marking it as a British film and of course in those
days British films were not really popular with people in
America. He wouldn't compromise in any way.*[15]

Balcon can be considered one of British cinema's *auteurs*,
not in the creative sense because he had no direct input into
either script or direction, but he was an impresario who was
able to raise the finance, supervise the production, assemble
the team and provide the environment that motivated
creativity. His authorship was underpinned by his documented
philosophy to make pictures 'which express England',[16] to
present the world 'with a complete picture of Britain'.[17]

His belief in British cinema extended beyond its function as
entertainment to its social and political role. The protection
of the British home market and his opposition to American
cultural imperialism were part of this philosophy. The status of
British cinema was dependent on British film-makers having
a duty to Britain; he was very critical of British colleagues
now working in the USA and particularly of Alfred Hitchcock
(who left Britain in 1939 to work for David O. Selznick) and
talked scornfully about him 'cavorting about in Hollywood'. His

apparent refusal to compromise was based on his belief that a true representation of Britishness would have appeal as a genuine product:

> I am sure we can get into the American market, but it will be with films of genuine British character. We shall become international by being national.[18]

From Birmingham to Ealing

Born in 1896, the year that moving pictures came to Britain, Michel Balcon first worked in Birmingham as a jeweller's apprentice. In 1915 he joined the Dunlop Rubber Company, becoming personal assistant to the managing director and gaining valuable experience of industrial practice and management. In 1921, together with Victor Saville (also from Birmingham), he moved to an office in London's Soho to set up a film distribution company, Victory Motion Pictures. They moved into production – Balcon, Freedman and Saville – with their first feature film *Woman to Woman* (dir. Graham Cutts, 1923) filmed at Islington studios and written by Cutts and the 24-year-old Alfred Hitchcock. Its success led to Balcon forming Gainsborough Pictures in 1924, making films at Islington. It was there that Balcon produced *The Pleasure Garden* in 1925, Alfred Hitchcock's first film as a director. In 1931 he took charge of production at Gaumont-British (Gainsborough's 'sister' company) at Lime Grove, Shepherds Bush. There he made a series of Hitchcock thrillers including *The Man Who Knew Too Much* (1934) and *The 39 Steps* (1935). His association with Hitchcock began his objective, so prominent in his time at Ealing, to promote 'people of unusual promise' from within his organisation. At Gaumont-British he had been introduced to the American Robert Flaherty, the so called 'father of the documentary film', and had given him

£10,000 to make *Man of Aran* (1934). This was a mixture of reality and fiction, with staged scenes which included a shark hunt in an area sharks no longer inhabited.

Shepherds Bush was one of the studios forced to close in the downturn of 1936 and Balcon went to MGM-British at Denham Studios. This was the British subsidiary of Metro-Goldwyn-Meyer, perhaps the most sophisticated, glamorous and star-studded studio in Hollywood. At first he saw his appointment as a 'heaven sent opportunity' to combine British writing and acting talent with 'Hollywood money, stars, distribution power and expertise'. This, however, came at a price. MGM was not prepared to surrender control over issues such as writing and casting. After completing *A Yank at Oxford* for MGM (directed by Jack Conway in 1938 and described by Geoff Brown as 'in a style far more Yank than Oxford'[20]) Balcon resigned and replaced Basil Dean as head of production for ATP. He began to issue films under the name of Ealing Studios.

8   See H. Mark Glancy, 'Hollywood and Britain: MGM and the British Quota Legislation', in Jeffrey Richards (ed.) (1998) *The Unknown 1930s: An Alternative History of the British Cinema 1929–1939*, p. 59.

9   Jonathan Glancey, 'The Mogul's Monuments', *The Guardian*, Saturday, 18 May 2002.

10   Jeffrey Richards, *Film and British National Identity, op. cit.*, p. 265.

11   *My Little Stick of Blackpool Rock* (1937) referred to a particular type of confectionery: '*it may be sticky but I never complain, it's nice to have a nibble at it now and again.*' A BBC memo stated 'certain lines in the lyric must not be broadcast'. The verse which gave particular offense appears to have been:
     '*With my little stick of Blackpool Rock, along the promenade I stroll.*
     In the ballroom I went dancing each night
     No wonder every girl that danced with me, stuck to me tight.'

12   He was knighted in 1948 for his services to the film industry.

13   Michael Balcon (1969) *Michael Balcon Presents... A Lifetime of Films*, London: Hutchinson, p. 53. In his ability to epitomise the values of his family's adopted country Balcon has been compared to the Hollywood Jewish Moguls such as the Warner Brothers (Harry, Albert, Samuel and Jack), Harry Cohn,

Marcus Loew and David Selznick. Andrew Higson has pointed out that some of the most 'English' films of the 1930s were made by the Hungarian Alexander Korda, another Jewish immigrant – e.g. *Sanders of the River* (dir. Zoltan Korda,1935 London Film Productions).

14   Jill Balcon interview in (1986) *Omnibus, 'Made in Ealing'*, *op. cit.*

15   Ronald Neame, *ibid.*

16   Michael Balcon (1931) 'Sincerity Will Make the Film English', *The Era* (London), 11 Nov 1931 as quoted in Brown (1984) 'A Knight and his Castle', in Brown and Kardish, *op. cit.*, p. 19.

17   Balcon interviewed in *Kinematograph Weekly*, 11 January 1945, p. 163 as quoted in Richards and Aldgate (1999) *Best of British: Cinema and Society 1930-1970*, London: I.B.Taurus, p. 99.

18   Interview with Molly Hobman, 'Mr Balcon's Film Plans', *Birmingham Gazette*, 23 July 1938 as quoted in Brown (1984) 'A Knight and his Castle', in Brown and Kardish, *op. cit.*, p. 27.

19   H. Mark Glancy in Richards, *The Unknown '30s, op. cit.*, p. 67.

20   Geoff Brown in Brown and Kardish, *op. cit.*, p. 26.

3. BALCON'S CELLULOID ENGLAND

Balcon's celluloid England was as he believed it to be, or wanted it to be, and how he wanted the audience to believe it. It was working/middle class, liberal, traditional, comfy, and parochial, with a strong sense of community where – when everybody pulled together – things usually worked out for the best. In other words, England was very much like his domain at Ealing. This is how Balcon saw it and that is how he managed his studio: as a democratic team with 'Mick' Balcon as head coach. **Adrienne Mancia**[21]

The Producer

Charles Barr has summed up Balcon's philosophy as 'small is beautiful, old is good' and Ealing did appear to be small when compared with the might of MGM. Balcon had no regrets about his decision to leave the major enterprise, his daughter Jill recalls him as saying: 'I'd rather run my own ship and sink with it if I have to than work for Louis B. Meyer.'[22] The glamour of the Hollywood monolith was exchanged for a small-scale 'little England' cottage industry, having, as Monja Danischewsky described it in 1938:

> [the] air of a family business...the administrative block which faced the green looked like a country cottage and was separated from the studios by a neat little rose garden.[23]

However charming the setting Balcon's tough business acumen, sharpened by six years in the tyre business and seventeen in the film industry, cannot be underestimated. If, in some respects, we are to consider him, as suggested, as the prime *auteur* of Ealing films (with all the debate that such a contention raises) there are two related strands to the argument which both arise out of his position as head of production: firstly, his ability to raise the necessary finance fundamental to getting the films made; and, secondly, David Puttnam's contention that 'The secret of Ealing's success lay in Balcon's ability to spot creative potential and invest in it.'[24] In a lecture given in 1945 to the British Film Institute Summer School on Film Appreciation Balcon outlined what he saw as the function of the Producer. His role was to make the final decisions on what projects to develop, obtain finance for the production and allocate the key creative roles. These two strands – finance and the ability to understand how best to use the team at his disposal – operated under the 'hands on' and then 'hands off' approach, the idea that 'as soon as the work on the studio floor commences the producer should step back to some extent'. His contention was:

> *A film producer is only as good as the sum total of the ability of his colleagues with whom he works, and in this respect I have been uniquely fortunate.* [25]

Finance and the Deal with Rank

> *He took all the burden of finance off our shoulders: once he had agreed to do something, he fought all the battles while we got on with making the films.* **Michael Relph**[26]

During the 1940s there were about forty British feature films made every year, and on average five of those were made at Ealing. The National Provincial Bank and Courtaulds provided about half the finance and in 1944 Balcon came to an agreement with the Rank Organisation, which had been created by J. Arthur Rank in 1937. This organisation had a vertically integrated hold on the industry in Britain and, if they were to counter the threat posed by Hollywood, needed to expand into the American and World market by securing the distribution of British films abroad. Rank owned 70% of all British studio space including Pinewood and Denham. He controlled General Film Distributors (the major British distributors) and the Odeon and Gaumont-British cinema chains and needed to invest in film production in order to ensure a supply of quality films to fill his cinemas. Apart from making their own films the Organisation had created Rank Independent Productions entering into distribution contracts with production teams such as The Archers (Powell and Pressburger) and Cineguild (David Lean, Ronald Neame, Anthony Havelock-Allen). The deal with Ealing guaranteed to provide some 50% (later 75%) finance, distribution of the films in Rank cinemas as 'A' features (the main film and top billing in a cinema programme) and Ealing's approval of the terms on which their films were booked. Ealing had access to the development, printing and optical processes at Rank's Denham laboratories and were also able to use actors that were under Rank contract.

Previously very scathing about the power of the so-called 'Oriental Potentates'[27] Balcon had managed to negotiate an exceptional arrangement which left Ealing financially stable but able to maintain complete creative control and independence. His shrewd understanding of the market was proved right when Rank persuaded him to step outside his usual territory and join their attempt at expansion into the international prestige film. *Saraband for Dead Lovers* (dir. Basil Dearden, 1948) was Ealing's first Technicolor film, a costume drama set in the 18th century English Court, with some of the locations shot in Prague. Its lavish art direction by William Kellner and Jim Morahan was nominated for an Oscar.

It was a box office failure and the Studio's costliest flop. Just over six months later Ealing released *Passport to Pimlico* (dir. Henry Cornelius, 1949), a low-budget black and white comedy about wartime rationing filmed partly on a Lambeth bomb site. Like most of the other low-budget comedies it covered all its costs and made money.

The Enclosed World of Ealing

> *All studios tend to be an enclosed world while a film is being made, but as far as Ealing was concerned, we lived in an enclosed world for a decade. That small studio was where we lived. That was its strength and weakness, I suppose.* **Sidney Cole** [28]

Over 400 people worked at Ealing Studios. These included a virtual repertory company of actors and a creative elite of about 50 on permanent contract, unusual even for the 1940s. The modest salaries earned by this elite (many of whom stayed at the studio for years) were the price they were willing to pay for guaranteed employment in a notoriously unstable industry, and the opportunity to 'get on with making the films' in what has been described as a family atmosphere. This atmosphere, so noticeable in any recollections of working at the studio,[29] had been initiated by Basil Dean in the 1930s. Dean had put up a notice 'The Studio with the Team Spirit', and had called the canteen 'The Inn'. The 'team spirit' was to continue, with 'The Inn' transferring to the Red Lion Public House situated opposite the studio entrance on the other side of the Green where, according to Michael Relph, a 'tremendous lot of drinking went on'.[30]

The spirit of consensual and democratic decision making was fostered not only by alcohol but also by the regular fortnightly meetings of key personnel around the Round Table in the Company Directors' dining room. Each unit presented a progress report on the project it was working on and discussed future projects. The proposals for films mostly originated in the script department or in ideas suggested by other members of staff, with only a small proportion (around 20% to 25%) adapted from plays or novels. Balcon, the benevolent autocrat, had ultimate authority in deciding what was made. Journalist Francis Koval observed one of the meetings for a *Sight and Sound Festival Special* in 1951:

> *Sir Michael Balcon conducted the discussion almost paternally, without any formality; and even the presence of a journalist did not seem to impose any restraint on the free flow of ideas or the raising of delicate questions.*[31]

Everyone was known by their first name or a nickname, although John Ellis has identified a hierarchy of four distinct social groups:

- The creative elite on permanent salaries – directors, screenwriters, editors, cinematographers.

- The permanent workers on wages (who often lived nearby) – technicians, secretaries.

- Temporary salaries – leading actors, outside screenwriters, composers.

- Temporary wages – minor roles, extras, technical advisors.

In this hierarchy the Ealing ethos was shaped by those in the first category. Ellis has noted that almost all the studio staff were from the comfortable middle class – some Oxbridge educated (Robert Hamer, T. E. B. Clarke, Charles Crichton,

Charles Frend). Alexander Mackendrick and Michael Relph came from art college, Basil Dearden from the theatre. Ellis comes to the conclusion that:

> The concentration of Ealing's films on the lower middle class is a result of a complex of factors. The first is biographical: the majority of the film-makers were born into middle class families, many strongly imbued with old fashioned liberalism, which expressed the class interest of the emergent lower sections of the bourgeoisie. They were of the generation which passed through the depression and were radicalised by it, producing a desire to show 'people' in films.[32]

They also had 'privileged access to knowledge and culture' and their isolated position 'could only concern "the people" as those groups at the lowest level of their own class: the petty bourgeois stratum of small shopkeepers and clerks'. They were famously given the name by Monja Danischewsky of 'Mr Balcon's Young Gentlemen'.

Mr Balcon's Academy for Young Gentlemen

> Balcon's limitations were also his strengths. He didn't make films. His raw material was not the film itself. His raw material was us. **Alexander Mackendrick**

> He ran Ealing like a minor public school. **Michael Relph** [33]

When studying Ealing Studios two of the key words used to describe the team that created the films are 'continuity' and 'stability'. Between 1938 and 1959 the Studio produced ninety-six films and sixty-two of those were directed by one of the permanent team:

- Basil Dearden: Twenty-one films from 1942 to 1956.

- Charles Frend: Twelve films from 1942 to 1957.

- Harry Watt: Six films from 1943 to 1959.

- Charles Crichton: Thirteen films from 1944 to 1957.

- Robert Hamer: Five films from 1945 to 1952.

- Alexander Mackendrick: Five films from 1949 to 1955.

Between 1942 and 1951 no director came from outside the studio. Promotions were made from within – Leslie Norman, Michael Truman and Seth Holt worked their way up to being directors. Films were mostly written by regular screenwriters T. E. B. Clarke, Angus McPhail, John Dighton and Jack Whittingham. Repertory performers included Jack Warner, Stanley Holloway, Sidney Tafler, Joan Greenwood, Alec Guinness, Jack Hawkins and Googie Withers.

'A Stamp of Quality'

Balcon stressed that some of the most important work was done on a film after shooting finished. At Ealing post-production culminated in the film posters, many of which are classics of British graphic design. Monja Danischewsky, who had worked as a journalist after studying at the Royal College of Art, was put in charge of publicity and in 1943 he appointed the painter, designer and art critic S. John Woods to supervise the artwork that advertised the films. Woods commissioned a small number of artists – including John Piper, John Minton, Edward Bawden, Leslie Hurry, James Boswell and Ronald Searle – and they produced art works that were very different to the usual posters of the day. Whereas Hollywood advertised their films with idealised figures of stars, the artists selected by Woods used their own individual style to depict the themes and essence of each film (such as Leslie Hurry for *Dead of Night*, James Boswell for *It Always Rains on Sunday* and Edward Bawden for *The Titfield Thunderbolt*). Monja Danischewsky summed it up when he wrote in 1966: 'One thing I am sure about is that the overall effect put a stamp of quality on the Ealing output as a whole.'[34]

The Product

Ealing films were mainly given 'U' certificates (Universal that could be watched by everyone). Lasting eighty to ninety minutes, they were made on tight budgets of around £120,000 to £200,000 with shooting schedules of eight to ten weeks. The budget did not allow for complicated camera movements that slowed down shooting so the 'Ealing style' largely consisted of static shots and short takes. The philosophy of realism, embedded in Ealing's response to the War, encouraged use of location and bland studio lighting rather than the strong contrasts between light and darl of *chiaroscuro*. Working within the strict parameters of finance, regulation, house style and ethos did not hamper individual expression and creativity and, it could be argued, it gave individual *auteurs* such as Robert Hamer and Alexander Mackendrick the secure boundaries that their ideas could push against.

As stated these boundaries that define the Ealing film had been cemented into place as a response to the conflict that faced Britain just after Balcon took over the studio. If we are to examine British cinema as having a distinctive national identity then the films made during the War are, ideologically as well as chronologically, the natural place to begin.

21   Adrienne Mancia (1984) in Brown and Kardish, *op. cit.*, p. 14.

22   Jill Balcon interviewed in *Forever Ealing* (2002) directed by Andrew Snell, broadcast on Channel 4. Louis B. Meyer was the head of the Hollywood studio.

23   Monja Danischewsky (1938) as quoted in Barr, *op. cit.*, p. 6.

24   David Putnam (1984) in Brown and Kardish, *op. cit.*, p. 7.

25   Michael Balcon (1945) *The Producer*, London: BFI, p. 7.

26   Michael Relph, producer, director, production designer and writer at Ealing in an interview with Robin Buss 'England's Dreaming', *The Independent*, Sunday, 25 July 1993.

27   Name given by Harold Wilson MP, President of the Board of Trade in a memo dated September 1949. He described Maxwell and Rank disparagingly as 'Oriental potentates' who dictated British film policy. By 1942 the Rank organisation owned 642 cinemas. The other cinema circuit, Associated British Cinemas (ABC) under John Maxwell, owned around 460.

28   Sidney Cole, producer and editor at Ealing, interviewed in Robin Buss 'England's Dreaming', *op. cit.*

29   'Denham was Buckingham Palace. Ealing was charming and small. When one said I'm working at Ealing, one could be sure that one was making an interesting film, usually a funny film, and most likely a good film. It had the best atmosphere of all the English studios I worked in,' Herbert Lom in an interview with Matthew Sweet, 'Ealing Studios: Kind Hearts and Funny Men', *The Independent*, Sunday, 28 July 2002.
'Ealing was a very special place. It wasn't a studio that people rented out and came and left and so on. Ealing was a home.' Sir Richard Attenborough (2002), interviewed in *Forever Ealing, op. cit.*

30   Michael Relph, interviewed by Robin Buss, 'England's Dreaming', *op. cit.*

31   Francis Koval as quoted in John Ellis, *op. cit.*, p. 93.

32   John Ellis, *op.cit.*, pp. 79–80.

33   Alexander Mackendrick and Michael Relph (1986) interviewed in *Made in Ealing, op. cit.*

34   Monja Daniscewsky (1966) *White Russian, Red Face* as quoted in Emmeline Leary, *Action! Comedy! Romance! Classic Film Posters from Ealing Studios*, Ealing Films Festival, 1989.

4. EALING AT WAR

The aim in making films during the War was easy enough to state but more difficult to achieve. It was, first and foremost, to make a good film, a film that people would want to see, and at the same time to make it honest and truthful and to carry a message, or an example, which would be good propaganda for morale and the war effort.

Michael Balcon [35]

When Balcon took over the Studio in 1938 he was already conscious to the fact that war was coming. He sent a memorandum to a Government department outlining his plans for 'the harnessing of films to the national effort'. As a film-maker and a patriot he began to formulate ways in which cinema could play its part in shaping attitudes as well as reflecting them during the time of conflict.

British Cinema during World War II

World War II began in September 1939. It had a big impact on British cinema, providing it with a special set of circumstances which initiated what has been seen as its Golden Age. Fewer British films were made but they were of better quality and enjoyed an unprecedented popularity. 'Going to the pictures' gave structure to a disrupted social life and films with their specifically British subject matter drew large audiences – the average weekly attendance, estimated at nineteen million in 1939, had risen to over thirty million by 1945.

From the outset of hostilities a blackout was put into operation and British cities were pitched into darkness. At first all cinemas and places of public entertainment were closed because of the threat of air raids but this was soon rescinded.

Politicians realised that entertainment was necessary to increase and sustain morale and that films were of great value as propaganda. Cinemas re-opened their doors. During the 1930s they had been places of escape from the everyday hardships of the Depression into a world of fantasy. Wartime audiences still enjoyed the fantasy (particularly during the last years when they were confident of victory), but films could also reassure them that their courage and endeavour would eventually triumph. Added to this was the fact that now the auditoria were warm enclosed spaces where people could shelter, where the presence of many others provided comfort and companionship. They presented spectators with a kind of normality when they left the blackness outside for the brightly lit world projected onto the screen.

Wartime British audiences had a keen sense of national identity fostered by a common enemy, shared experiences and purpose. Cinema helped in the construction of a 'nation united by adversity', with a sense of community and co-operation. Films had to be made with the same restrictions that operated on other manufacturing industries with personnel conscripted, studios requisitioned and photographic materials and equipment often in short supply. They were also subject to the restrictions and censorship of all other forms of communication. In spite of this Ealing, one of the three major studios to continue during the War, expanded their film production in response to the national need.

Cinema as Propaganda and the Documentary Style

As soon as the War began, the Government recruited members of the intelligentsia 'to present the national case to the public at home and abroad' by forming the Ministry of Information (MOI). Its remit was both to operate an information policy, censoring 'as may be demanded by the needs of security' and to produce propaganda. The MOI Films Division took over the General Post Office Film Unit (GPO) in order to produce War documentaries, renaming it the Crown Film Unit. It also laid down guidelines for commercial film producers to make films, running an Ideas Committee to formulate film scenarios. They operated a form of pre-censorship where scripts were presented for inspection. If these were approved film stock was made available and actors and other film personnel were released from military service. At first films were vehicles for War propaganda but by 1942 the MOI realised that entertainment could also be used for the same purpose. The emphasis should however always be placed on the 'positive virtues of British characteristics and the democratic way of life'.[36]

Balcon's relationship with the MOI was erratic. He conflicted with officials about what he felt was an appropriate national style and how this could best be used to further the cause of victory. His belief was that such a national style existed in the British Documentary Movement, established by John Grierson in the late 1920s. The films made by bodies such as the Empire Marketing Board and the GPO Film Unit were supported by the State, and therefore untainted by commercial considerations, with film units given a large amount of creative freedom. They were serious and committed forms of education and instruction, the subjects of the films were of social significance featuring 'real' people in 'real' locations. Realism conferred a moral superiority as opposed to the 'tinsel' of mere entertainment, becoming the cornerstone of Balcon's Ealing ethos. In a lecture given in 1943 to the Workers' Film Association he quoted from a leading article in Documentary News Letter:

...it must be to the point that men and women welcome the idea of living in a real world. It is only by knowing it truly and honestly that they can work and play in it happily. With knowledge of the real world they can have such a full life that all of man's heaven from Mount Olympus to Hollywood, Calif. will seem as less than the dreary emptiness of a ballroom in the morning sunlight. People will see that the world itself is rich enough and noble enough to provide for all their needs.[37]

Film-makers with experience of the movement could bring their expertise to the feature film, which would not be about artificial histrionics but restrained reality. *Convoy* (dir. Pen Tennyson) released in July 1940, was the first of the Ealing films to feature the War directly. It was:

Dedicated in all gratitude to the Officers and Men of the Royal and Merchant Navy. Their cheerful co-operation made it possible to present the many scenes in our film which were taken at sea under wartime conditions.

Balcon was to comment on the film in 1943 that:

The balance between the strictly documentary and the story elements in this new type of film is still the most difficult thing to achieve... .Cameramen were sent out with convoys and much authentic material was obtained and, what is more strange, actually used in the final film. I was very happy about Convoy *at the time as indeed I had every reason to be. It had a great success, both as regards prestige and returns, and was even referred to in the House of Commons as fine propaganda for the Navy.[38]*

Documentary elements using film footage shot in the North Sea brought the necessary sobriety to a propaganda film that sought to entertain (it was a box office success and was released in the USA). *Convoy* was a film about officers, with a romantic triangle plot featuring characters from that class. If, however, they were to embrace the true spirit of the British documentary style laid down by Grierson as 'the drama of the doorstep' film-makers needed to produce a more coherent and inclusive view of Britain. The formulation of such a documentary drama style was cemented by two directors who left the GPO Unit in the early 1940s to work for Balcon at Ealing: Alberto Cavalcanti and Harry Watt.

Alberto Cavalcanti, Reality + Art

Of all the group there [at Ealing] I would say that Cavalcanti was the most important to talk to and work with. **Michael Balcon**[39]

Alberto Cavalcanti was a Brazilian who studied architecture in Switzerland and then went to Paris in the 1920s where he designed sets for the experimental film-maker Marcel l'Herbier. His first film as director was the highly stylised *Rien que les Heures* (1926), the first of the 'city symphonies' of the 1920s. Between 1927 and his move to Britain in 1934 he made twenty features and short films, part of the first *avant garde* of French cinema. In Britain he headed the GPO Film Unit, directing thirteen documentaries including *Coalface* (1935) and acting as sound director on *Night Mail* (dir. Harry Watt and Basil Wright, 1936).

He brought with him to Ealing the experiences gained in these two different environments – the sophisticated, experimental and sometimes disruptive European *avant garde* and the committed actuality of the British Documentary Movement. As supervisor and trainer to the young film-makers who became part of the Ealing team he can be seen as crucial to the way that their work developed.

Cavalcanti acted as associate producer for *The Foreman Went to France* (dir. Charles Frend, 1942). This derived from a story by J. B. Priestley based on an actual wartime incident. The film represents a change of emphasis for Ealing, a film about war that features ordinary working men and women rather than heroic servicemen. A Welsh factory foreman undertakes a mission to recover a vital piece of machinery his firm has installed in France, so that it will not fall into the hands of the enemy. He is helped by three people from different backgrounds: two British soldiers, one a cockney (Tommy) and one a Scot (Jock), and an American girl. The three men, embodiments of the unified British Isles, are helped by their female ally (the USA entered the War in December 1941) and show their solidarity with the French (France was occupied by the Germans from 1940). This collaboration allows the group to overcome the obstacles that stand in their way, including a British officer who is really working for the enemy. This move away from the stoicism and stiff upper lip of the earlier films towards the bravery and initiative of ordinary citizens and the possible treachery of those who are in privileged positions was to be the subject of Cavalcanti's first Ealing film as director.

Went the Day Well?

> *People of the kindest character, such as the people in that small English village, as soon as the War touches them, become absolutely monsters.* **Alberto Cavalcanti**[40]

One of the most powerful films made during the war *Went the Day Well?* (dir. Alberto Cavalcanti, 1942) was filmed in 1942 just after the fall of Singapore, when the threat of a German invasion was very real. This invasion would be possible from outside the British Isles if the enemy were aided by traitors inside. The audience were used to messages about public vigilance and warnings against complacency: 'Careless talk costs lives.' In this film people are not what they seem – English soldiers are Germans, Squire Wilsford is a traitor and seemingly placid citizens can become ferocious partisans. *The Lieutenant Died Last*, the story on which it is based, had been written by Graham Greene in 1940 to persuade the Americans to enter the War by showing them how resilient the British were and how they deserved support. The MOI did not sponsor the project but supported the film by giving permission for troops from the Gloucestershire Regiment to act as soldiers.

The setting is a pretty English village that could adorn a chocolate box – old cottages, Manor House, Vicarage, old church – inhabited by villagers who conform to the accepted social hierarchy: aristocratic squire, lady of the manor, vicar and his spinster daughter, seaman on leave, postmistress, policeman, poacher, cheeky cockney evacuee. The Home Guard ride bicycles, the outside world does not disturb the genteel tranquillity and the War is far away. The village is a little island surrounded by peaceful countryside. Its insularity appears at first to be its strength but turns out to be its weakness. It can suddenly be isolated, violently disrupted, invaded by a ruthless enemy who can only be defeated by an equally ruthless and united population.

The film begins in documentary fashion accompanied by William Walton's stirring music. A travelling shot along country roads through English countryside takes us into a quiet churchyard in the village of Bramley End. It is the future, the War is over and the British have been victorious. Charles Sims, the gravedigger and church warden, directly

Went the Day Well? – *The direct address of the documentary*

addresses the camera and the spectator: 'Come to have a look at Bramley End have you?' It is a place of tradition and history, mentioned in the Doomsday Book. He shows us the tombstones of German soldiers: 'They wanted England those Jerries did, and this is the only bit they got.' In a structure similar to that of *The Foreman Went to France* we are told the outcome before the narrative flashes back to May 1942. German soldiers disguised as members of the British Army take over the village. The spectator knows who they are but the villagers are deceived, as they are by the Squire who we learn is a traitor. The villagers defer to him through his status as a member of the ruling class and therefore their natural leader. The picture of the aristocracy as quislings may have resonated with an audience who had read about the Duke of Windsor's meeting with Hitler before the war and the pro-Nazi sympathies of other members of the British aristocracy such as Unity and Diana Mitford. The casting of Leslie Banks as Squire Oliver Wilsford was a masterstroke as audiences associated him with Governor Sanders in *Sanders of the River* (dir. Zoltan Korda, 1935 London Films), the paternal upright figure who had saved the British Empire by quelling the threat from African tribes who dared to question his authority.

At first the villagers of Bramley End are welcoming and completely unsuspecting, but gradually their suspicions are aroused. When this happens the film erupts into ferocious violence as the true nature of the enemy becomes clear. The Germans can now shed their veneer of civilisation and bayonet the postmistress, ambush and slaughter the unsuspecting Home Guard and shoot the Vicar in his church as he attempts to ring the bell to warn of the occupation. The retaliation of the characters that have been presented to us as good natured is uncompromising as they too shed their own thin covering of civilised behaviour and learn to kill. The Vicar's daughter

Retaliation – middle aged ladies hack men to death with axes

Nora, the repressed spinster attracted to the Squire, has been doubly deceived. She reacts to his treachery and betrayal by acting as his executioner. Her actions are part of the uncharacteristic female brutality, potential for aggression and heroism in seemingly restrained women that is such a shocking factor in the film. Middle aged ladies hack men to death with axes, young women shoot to kill as in some fairground game; the upper class lady of the manor sacrifices herself for a group of cockney children. As well as the female characters representing what would be considered as displaying unstereotypical traits the film also attributes real heroism to the lower ranks – the village poacher and the cockney evacuee. The screenplay was written by resident writers Angus MacPhail, John Dighton and Diana Morgan – the only woman writer at Ealing.

Went the Day Well? broke the mould of the British War film. Cavalcanti himself saw it as an anti-war film where an ordered society is disrupted by a violent enemy and forced to resort to its own suppressed violence. Its representation of the 'English people', though unusual in its depiction of class and gender, drew praise from film critic Dilys Powell in *The Sunday Times*:

> *For once the English people are shown as capable of individual and concentrated resourcefulness in a fight and not merely steady in disaster....The essential virtue of the film is its expression of an English tradition: the tradition of the rural community, self contained... still drawing strength from the past, still adding to its own experience to the common store of village history... .At last, it seems, we are learning to make films with our own native material.*[41]

Her comments can perhaps be seen in the light of a Britain mobilised by War and having to examine itself and its values. In documentaries made by Humphrey Jennings in the same period the highest praise is reserved for 'a peoples' army of volunteers ... they are the ones who are really fighting this war' (*London Can Take It*, 1940 Crown Film Unit). The message in *The Heart of Britain* (1941 Crown Film Unit) was also very clear:

> *These people are slow to anger, not easily roused. These people have the power to hit back and the Nazis will learn once and for all that no one with impunity troubles the heart of Britain.*

Went the Day Well? abandons all the restraint usually associated with British patriotism and depicts such a community as a collective hero activated and ready to retaliate.

San Demetrio, London

A unified team singing together

This change in emphasis can also be seen in *San Demetrio, London* (dir. Charles Frend, 1943), an example of a drama given status by its documentary feel – 'the story came from the news'. Dedicated to 'The Officers and Men of the British Merchant Navy' the script, written by Robert Hamer and Charles Frend, uses firsthand accounts of the actual incident which had taken place in the winter of 1940 during some of the darkest days of the War when the British Isles were virtually under siege and naval convoys provided the lifeline for vital supplies. The *San Demetrio*, an oil tanker carrying aviation fuel from Texas back to the beleaguered British Isles, is part of a convoy attacked in the mid-Atlantic. The crew are forced to abandon the burning tanker because of the danger of explosion. One group, consisting of the Second Officer, the Chief Engineer, a handful of assorted merchant seamen (including a Scot, a Welshmen and an Irishman) and an alcoholic bragging American ('you need somebody's help to win this War') drift for some time in great discomfort in tempestuous seas. Their drift brings them full circle back to the burning *San Demetrio*, and they collectively take the decision to re-board the ship rather than remain in the flimsy and exposed lifeboat. Once on board they have to work together to put out the fires, start the damaged engines and steer the ship back to the British Isles without charts or compasses. The decision to do this is arrived at in democratic fashion, a reflection of the desire that a more egalitarian Britain would emerge after the War. The triumph over adversity is possible with a unified team to which everybody contributes, symbolised (as in Humphrey Jennings' *Fires were Started* made the same year) by the men singing together. Preston the American, now fully integrated as a vital contributor to the effort, joins in. His essential involvement is recognised at the end of the film by the award of the ships tattered Red Ensign. The conclusion recognises 'courage, devotion and sacrifice... the very modest recital of some gallant gentlemen concerning a memorable achievement'. The war was no longer being fought solely by the military but was a 'people's war' and films were an essential part of the construction of its ideology.

35   Michael Balcon (1969) *Michael Balcon Presents....A Lifetime of Films*, *op. cit.*, p. 148.

36   *Kinematograph Weekly*, 30 July 1942, as quoted in Aldgate and Richards (1986) *Britain Can Take It: The British Cinema in the Second World War*, Edinburgh: Edinburgh University Press, p. 12.

37   Michael Balcon (1943) *Realism or Tinsel?*, from Monja Danischewsky (ed.) (1947) *Michael Balcon's 25 Years in Films*, London World Film Publications, p. 72. [Query: place/city of publisher?]

38   *Ibid.*, p. 71.

39   Balcon as quoted in Elizabeth Sussex, 'Cavalcant in England', in *Sight and Sound* 44(4), Autumn 1975.

40   Alberto Cavalcanti (1975), interview with Elizabeth Sussex in *Sight and Sound, op. cit.*

41   Dilys Powell, *The Sunday Times*, 1 November 1942.

5. BRITAIN ON THE EDGE 1: An Isolated Experiment

Britain after the War: A Programme for Change

During the immediate post-war years there was a great desire for major social changes and reforms. The Labour Government (1945–51) led by Clement Atlee was elected on such a programme. They began the nationalisation of the key industries of coal, electricity, transport, gas, iron and steel. They created the Welfare State bringing in legislation that broadly carried out the ideals of the Beveridge Report, which had been written in 1942 and promised to the suffering population as future recompense for wartime hardships. The suggested reforms included the establishment of a National Health Service and a national system of benefits which would provide social security protecting the population from the 'cradle to the grave'. It became the responsibility of the State to tackle the 'Five Giant Evils on the road to reconstruction ...Disease, Ignorance, Squalor, Idleness and Want'. As well as changes within the British Isles there were also events outside which impacted on Britain as a nation. The granting of independence to India in 1947 and to Burma and Ceylon in 1948 began the breakup of the British Empire and the gradual erosion of British position and influence as a major colonial power.

The War had fostered a large audience for British films as the cinema was still the main form of entertainment. By 1946 cinema admissions had risen to an annual 1,635 million. This audience was one that been through an extraordinary six years and were having to cope with returning to a world where they had defeated the enemy but they were still in the midst of rationing and austerity. The devastating effects of civilian and military deaths, disruption to family life, bombing, loss of production, uncertainty and shortages allowed few material benefits from the victory and much real hardship as firsthand accounts testify:

> *The country was bankrupt. We had to face the cruellest winter anybody could remember, with little coal to heat our houses – if we had a house, that is.... Food rationing was stricter than at the lowest ebb of the war. Even bread was rationed and, for the first time ever in this country, horsemeat was on offer as a supplement to the meagre diet.*[42]

The move to a post-war society raised issues mostly subsumed during the conflict. Class hostility, apparently suspended when the enemy was the Nazis and everyone pulled together for the common good, surfaced again as Britain returned back to civilian life, being reconstructed with both the hopes of change and fears of different values. Ealing films articulated the anxieties that the changes generated in various ways – by diffusing them through laughter or continuing on their realist path and examining the contemporary social environment. There was also another way that the Studio tried only once – their sole venture into the horror genre. Once they saw what was inside that particular Pandora's Box they quickly closed it.[43]

Dead of Night

> *That's just what you need darling. It'll help you get rid of those horrible nightmares.*[44]

Dead of Night (dir. Basil Drearden, Robert Hamer, Alberto Cavalcanti and Charles Crichton, 1945) was made during the last months of the War and released just days after it ended. The film has often been cited as an atypical Ealing product, an isolated and unrepeated experiment which, as Charles Barr says, 'lifts the lid on forces of sex, violence and fantasy which Ealing's wartime project had kept almost out of sight'.[45] In 1945 horror was indeed an uncommon genre for a British film but there were political reasons for this. The ban on the distribution of horror films, imposed by the British Board of Film Censors and the Central Office of Information in 1942, had only just been lifted. Fears about the working classes (particularly working class males) being unable to handle the depiction of dark forces in darkened cinemas were based on the assumption that these forces might germinate 'unnatural passions' in those not educated or intelligent enough to repress them.

Dead of Night follows the convention of the *telling* of ghost stories. Telling requires a story teller and the framing narrative unites the experiences of five narrators in one of the earliest examples of the portmanteau horror film. It unfolds as a succession of stories in which the individual neuroses and obsessions that lie behind the characters' well-bred façades are personalised through the use of different voices. Five different writers contributed to the script, and four men were responsible for the direction. For Charles Barr this called to mind 'a session of the Ealing Round table, with individuals "submitting" stories in succession to the dreamer ... and the psychiatrist ... then joining in discussion.'[46]

Walter Craig, the central character who has previously 'dreamed' the story is also the spectator who, along with the audience, watches his nightmare being played out. The five narrators function to disseminate and control the narrative and the reactions of both Craig and the spectator. The individual stories all conform to the traditional elements of introduction, revelation, denouement not only within the individual episodes but also within the overall structure of the film. In this structure the dark forces play out with varying emphases – in turn the bizarre, the melancholic, the highly disturbing, the comic and the truly terrifying.

The doctor in the first story observes 'that apparition of death is what we call a psychological crisis'. One of the main themes of the film is dual identity and 'the return of the repressed', individual desires displaced onto a monstrous other coming back to their original source. This concept is central to Craig's dream and present in all the stories in some form. The schism of the real world with the world of nightmares had surely been broken as the War drew to its close. In the aftermath of the trauma the film-makers and the audience had to try to come to terms with the atrocities that had been perpetrated, such as the discovery of the Nazi extermination camps at Majdanek in July 1944 and Auschwitz in January 1945. Ealing's prevailing ethos during the War had been that of reconstructing the 'real' world, now revealed as capable of plunging into the depths of terrifying and only too real horrors.

The film begins with a drive along a country lane – this is the Home Counties, filmed in Stoke Poges and Turville (echoes of *Went the Day Well?* where dark events also overtook the apparent tranquillity). A contemporary setting was seen by writer M. R. James to be an essential component of horror fiction as 'to bring the fear home'.

The occupant of the car, architect Walter Craig, appears somewhat disturbed. He arrives at an isolated farmhouse, invited there for the weekend to design additions to the accommodation, and is greeted by the owner, Elliot Foley, and his mother with all the contained politeness and offers of tea of the English middle classes. The agitation that has been apparent from the beginning is intensified when Craig is introduced to the other guests who include Dr van Straaten, a European psychiatrist who refuses to believe in that they are all characters in Craig's recurring dream, dismissing it with a scientific, rational explanation that 'recurring dreams are quite common'.[48] The guests, however, begin to reveal strange and disturbing experiences one by one, all featuring either death or attempted murder. The first story, 'The Hearse Driver' (dir. Basil Dearden), opens the sequence with a bizarre tale. Hugh Grainger, a racing driver, is hospitalised after an accident. He flirts with his nurse and starts to read when he should be sleeping. It is night but his clock says 4.15 and when he goes to the window it is day. Outside is a hearse with a driver who beckons him with 'Just room for one more inside sir'. When released from hospital he waits for a bus. The time is 4.15 and the bus driver is the same sinisterly cheerful man 'Just room for one more inside sir'. Grainger watches as the bus plummets off a bridge. In this story Craig's own situation is underlined – Grainger's prophetic dreams are being experienced as an unexplained 'reality', relieved by what horror writer H. P. Lovecraft called 'touches of homely and prosaic detail'.[49]

'The Christmas Party' (dir. Alberto Cavalcanti) introduces a different visual style and the more Gothic tone of the Old Dark House. It is young ingénue Sally O'Hara's story. She attends a party where the guests all play Hide and Seek. Trying to shake off Johnny's attentions she gives him the slip. In an attic room she is alerted by the sobs of a child wearing a high ruffled collar. She comforts him as he tells her about his sister who hates him. Sally subsequently learns that the child is a ghost, murdered in the last century by his half sister who strangled him and then slit his throat. Sally's relentlessly cheerful demeanour, like that of the other guests, appears to have been little affected by this experience, but Craig's terror increases.

The return of the Gothic past

The most celebrated of the stories, 'The Haunted Mirror', continues the theme of the return of the Gothic past but here shifting its emphasis away from the discovery of a murdered child to the discovery of a murderous instinct within a seemingly normal man. The first film directed by Robert Hamer it is told by Joan Cortland, the character who seems the most sympathetic to Craig. The antique mirror is a gift from the energetic, positive yet controlled Joan to her rather limp, self-satisfied but equally controlled fiancé Peter: 'I thought you'd like to look at yourself.' Peter begins to see not his own languid reflection and that of his modern light apartment but a menacing other self in a dark Victorian bedroom with an ornate four-poster bed and a burning fire. His reaction echoes that of the spectator when confronted with horrific images: 'The only thing to do is try not to look at it, but in a queer sort of way it fascinates me.' His marriage to Joan (which he tries unsuccessfully to postpone) appears to dispel the images but when she goes away to visit her mother his menacing doppelgänger reappears. We learn, with Joan, the mirror's story as told by the owner of the antique shop: in the 19th century the mirror belonged to a domineering man who suffered a paralysing accident, and 'the effects of such constraint on a man of such enormous energy' led him to strangle his wife and watch himself in the mirror as he cut his own throat. This constrained energy has infected Peter, turning his lethargy into a raging sexual jealousy. His attempt to strangle Joan can only be stopped by her smashing the mirror, destroying his reanimated passions. According to David Pirie the mirror has acted:

> *As a kind of gateway through which all the psychological forces of imagination, sensuality and violence gradually erupt into the couple's repressed and artificial world.*[50]

Pirie's contention suggests that the placid and polite British exteriors hide a mass of base emotions which the mirror, the dream, the ghost story and the horror film allow the spectator to contemplate in relative safety.

'The Golfing Story' (dir. Charles Crichton) would appear to be much lighter in tone, as indeed it is, but it continues the theme of return from the dead in comic fashion, providing the spectator with the narrative pause which allows them to let down their guard, the light relief before the final onslaught. Basil Radford and Naunton Wayne reprise their double act first seen in *The Lady Vanishes* (dir. Alfred Hitchcock, 1938 Gainsborough Pictures). Stereotypical bumbling Englishmen, they are obsessed with 'playing the game' (in this case golf) and embarrassed by sex. When they are both drawn to the same woman they compete for her in a game of golf. Parratt cheats and wins, Potter drowns himself in the lake but comes back as a ghost with the promise to hang around and only disappear if Parratt will give up Mary (to which his friend agrees with alacrity) and also give up golf ('Never! I shall have nothing left to live for'). Unable to remember the sign ritual that dispatches him to the other world, Potter is still there on his friend's wedding night. Fondling a golfing trophy instead of his bride Parratt's consummation of his marriage is delayed until, trying to show Potter the disappearing ritual, he vanishes himself, leaving the ghost to satisfy Mary. The whimsical tone of this story, basically that of inhibited upper class English public schoolboys who are really only at ease with each other, forms a light comic relief that lulls Craig and the spectator into a feeling of security before plunging them both into the unrelieved darkness of the remainder of the film.

The story that follows, 'The Ventriloquist's Dummy' (dir. Alberto Cavalcanti), is also about a close male relationship. The sceptical Doctor van Straaten begins to relate a past case history before handing over his narration to the voice of Sylvester Kee, an American ventriloquist who has survived a murder attempt by another ventriloquist, the neurotic Maxwell Frere. The voice and actions of the dummy in such a performance are controlled by the performer, but Frere's dummy Hugo appears to be undermining that control. Frere is being taken over by another malevolent presence, just as Peter Cortland was taken over. Like Peter, Frere becomes ferociously jealous: 'I can't bear anyone touching him.' He believes that Kee is trying to steal Hugo, and when he finds the dummy in Kee's hotel bedroom he attempts to shoot the American. Van Straaten takes back the story and recounts his visit to the crazy Frere in prison where, at his suggestion, ventriloquist and dummy are reunited. This reunification is that of a suspicious lover with his fickle partner. When Hugo tells him he is leaving him to go to Kee Frere smothers the object of his love, and then destroys him by stamping on his head. Van Straaten and Kee visit the catatonic Frere in the asylum. The voice that he struggles to produce is that of Hugo – 'I've been waiting for you.'

The psychiatrist as spectator – Frere and Hugo are reunited

Walter Craig's nightmare moves inexorably towards its climax in spite of reassurances from Foley that 'there's nothing to be afraid of'. Left alone with van Straaten who can no longer see (having refused to see throughout the film) because his glasses have been broken, Craig acts on his compulsion 'to kill someone who has done me no harm' and strangles the psychiatrist. This breaks the logical progression of the narrative as it turns into an illogical nightmare montage of madness. He enters into the stories of his fellow guests, taking part in the Hide and Seek, begging to be let into the mirror, striking Sally senseless and encountering Hugo (now with Kee). Thrown into a prison cell with the dream characters crowded outside as spectators, Craig and the audience watch in terror as Hugo advances on him.

The split between the world of normality and that of the nightmare is signified by a track out with the image finally framed by an expanse of black screen. This fades into a bland modern well-lit bedroom, a cheerful wife enters and the phone is ringing, wakening a seemingly unperturbed Craig. The call is from Elliot Foley inviting him to spend the weekend at Pilgrim Farm to talk over the alterations he wishes to make and, as Craig says, to do a 'reconstruction job'. Instead of a reassuring closure the opening of the film repeats itself over the end credits but now we know what waits. The circular, never ending structure, will replay again and again, like the film.[51]

---

42 1940s Hard Times in Post-War Britain: When we didn't have it so good' @ http://bygonederbyshire. co.uk/articles/1940s: Hard_times_in_post war_Dritain.

43 The territory of sex and violence that they so firmly shut the door on in 1945 and only allowed to be opened by mavericks like Hamer and Mackendrick was to be successfully occupied by Hammer Studios from the mid 1950s, after Ealing had stopped production. Hammer's organisation in many ways parallels that of Ealing, with a second generation immigrant (Sir James Carreras) as head of the studio, a number of repertory performers, a regular creative team and a designated production base at Bray in Berkshire.

44 Mrs Craig to her husband Walter at the end of the film when he goes off to (re)visit the house in the country.

45 Charles Barr (1986) 'Introduction: Amnesia and Schizophrenia', in Barr (ed.) *All Our Yesterdays*, London: BFI, p.18.

46 Charles Barr, *Ealing Studios*, *op. cit.*, p.187.

46 M. R. James, *Some Remarks on Ghost Stories*, originally published in *The Bookman*, Christmas Issue, December 1929.

48 Recurring psychiatrists were also quite common: 1945 was a fruitful year for them in both British and Hollywood films. They proved a good way for the narrative to reveal what really lay behind the characters' search for identity. In Britain Ann Todd was cured by Herbert Lom in *The Seventh Veil* (dir. Compton Bennett, Ortus Films) and in Hollywood Ingrid Bergman showed that a female psychiatrist could play detective in *Spellbound* (dir. Alfred Hitchcock, USA Selznick International Pictures). What all psychiatrists have in common is of course their foreign (European) accent.

49 H. P. Lovecraft, *Supernatural Horror in Literature*, first published in The Recluse, 1927.

49 David Pirie (2008) *A New Heritage of Horror: The English Gothic Cinema*, London: I.B.Taurus, p. 18.

49 Or the Universe. According to IMDB: 'Cosmolgists Fred Hoyle, Thomas Gold and Hermann Bondi developed the Steady State theory of the Universe, an alternative to the Big Bang, after seeing *Dead of Night*. They said that the circular nature of the plot inspired the theory.'

50 David Pirie (2008) *A New Heritage of Horror: The English Gothic Cinema*, London: I.B.Taurus, p. 18 repeated.

51 Or the Universe. According to IMDB: 'Cosmolgists Fred Hoyle, Thomas Gold and Hermann Bondi developed the Steady State theory of the Universe, an alternative to the Big Bang, after seeing *Dead of Night*. They said that the circular nature of the plot inspired the theory.'

6. BRITAIN ON THE EDGE 2: Passions and Repressions

It Always Rains on Sunday

> *What we see is a morally bankrupt microcosm of post-WWII society, where most characters grab what they can, with no regard for anyone else. Tensions between notions of decency, and of family... permeate the film.*
>
> **David Sharp** [52]

Dead of Night was well received by critics (although some of the popular press appear to have called for it to be banned) and well liked by the public. The critics recognised that it was quality cinema, with particular contributions by Douglas Slocombe (cinematography) and Georges Auric (composer).[53] Two years later *It Always Rains on Sunday* (dir.Robert Hamer, 1947), also had music by Auric and atmospheric cinematography by Slocombe. The middle class world of *Dead of Night* was replaced with a picture of working class Londoners, living out what the *Monthly Film Bulletin* called: 'A sordid and dreary affair.... It is, perhaps, a pity that thousands of honest cheerful citizens of Bethnal Green could not have had a stronger representation.'[54] The Cinematograph Exhibitors Association pronounced it 'an unsavoury film... with appeal only to those with very broad minds'.[55] It was given an 'A' certificate (children had to be accompanied by an adult). Like *Dead of Night*, however, the film was popular with the public (the *Daily Mail* cited it as one of the top films of 1947) and we can now consider it as an example of British 40s cinema at its finest and central to any appraisal of Hamer as a tragic *auteur*:

> *This is clearly the work of a tortured soul. A repressed homosexual and a drunk, Hamer made six more features*

after Kind Hearts *without ever equalling that film's popular success or* Sunday's *artistic one. ....But for bad luck and a penchant for self-destructiveness, Hamer might have been one of the major figures in modern British cinema. As things stand,* It Always Rains on Sunday *is a major work, badly in need of rediscovery.* **Scott Foundas** [56]

Sunday routine

Those who praised the film for its realism recognised it as an authentic picture of 24 hours in the life of a group of working class characters living in the East End of London and readjusting to life two years after the War. The London of 1947 is one of restrictions, rationing, bomb damage, routine and poverty. The settings provide the spaces within which the characters' lives are shaped – the cramped terrace house near the railway line with the Anderson bomb shelter in the yard, the bar at the Two Compasses Public House, the seedy men's lodging house, Morry's record shop, the dance hall, the Sunday street market. Hamer was following the Studio's realist style but the authenticity of the settings goes beyond superficial duplication. Art director Duncan Sutherland created them as a 'presentation of a slice of life which would be recognisable to most members of the audience'. This 'slice of life' was praised by Dilys Powell for its accuracy:

*It Always Rains on Sunday has an amused, a devoted
attention to the tiny decorations of the everyday, to the
chattering neighbour, the darts game and the black cat
brushed with an exasperated gesture off the sofa head.
These trifles mark the difference between the studio set
and the room lived in: and an audience convinced of the
realism of the scene it watches becomes submissive to the
movement of the story.*[57]

The tone of the film is pessimistic, Andrew Pulver describes
it as 'one of British cinema's more successful stabs at
hardboiled *noir*'.[58] This is reflected in Douglas Slocombe's
moody cinematography with its contrasts between the flatly
lit restricted interiors and the low key rain-washed exteriors,
climaxing in the police hunt for Tommy in the railway
marshalling yards. Slocombe remarked on the look that
Hamer wanted, shooting at night with the mystery and drama
of light reflected off wet and metallic surfaces. This moves the
entire film away from realism and authenticity into what Scott
Foundas describes as a:

*....state of high anxiety – not a frame is wasted. Finally,
day gives way to night, the despair thickens, and all
points converge on a fever-dream train-yard finale of
long shadows, deep focus, billowing smoke, and rear
projection.*[59]

The working class location, *noir* lighting and characters on
the edge of society have been seen as reflecting affinities that
Hamer has with the European styles of French Poetic Realism
and Italian Neorealism (*Bicycle Thieves*, directed by Vittorio
de Sica, was made the year after, in 1948). The working class
are not presented as comic relief, nor are they patronised.
This totally unsentimental depiction predates the British
social realist dramas of the late 1950s and 1960s and, in its

depiction of the plurality of British identity, it foreshadows more contemporary British films. Centring on Bethnal Green this was the East End, home to a large Jewish community in the late 1940s – British citizens who eat stuffed olives and use Yiddish slang (Hamer had a particular interest in the use of language). Reviewing the film in 2008 for *The Jewish Week, New York* George Robinson praised it for going against a stereotypical single aspect representation:

> *All the Jewish characters, which run the gamut from a petty criminal and his would-be musical star brother to their social worker sister and their warm and affectionate father, are seen as fully realized, three-dimensional human beings. ...Perhaps one of the reasons that* It Always Rains on Sunday *is so generous to its Jewish characters is the fact that producer Michael Balcon and co-screenwriter Henry Cornelius were both Jews.*[60]

This depiction of a community going about their daily lives forms the backdrop to the central story, the return of something from the past to upset what could be described as the existing busy equilibrium of a normal present. This normality of the everyday is shattered by the reawakening of a dormant passion, which as Charles Barr notes: 'forces its way back, but in distorted and destructive forms, and there is no alternative but to stamp it out'.[61] The return of Rose's repressed feelings take us back to the mirror sequence of *Dead of Night* (underlined by the fact that Googie Withers plays both Joan Cortland and Rose), in spite of the fact that the two worlds appear to be very different.

The boredom of routine and the frustration that come with the struggle against poverty are underlined by the narrative, which begins and ends in the early morning where the gates of Whitechapel Underground Station are locked and the characters are enclosed in their neighbourhood. Within these 24 hours some will try to break free of the routine, dreaming of the past or of escape from the present. They are trapped – by their social circumstances, by home and family, by the law, by the rain – and the narrative will end where it began. They will be brought back to the real world, a world they must now accept.

The screenwriters (Angus MacPhail, Robert Hamer and Henry Cornelius) use a system of multiple parallel narratives that present us with an interlocking community of characters and events. The tag line used to promote the film – 'The secrets of a street you know' – suggests affinity with a TV soap opera in its melodramatic format and various personal dilemmas and temptations. Within the first fifteen minutes we have been introduced to several interconnecting strands:

1. Early Sunday morning. Coronet Grove, a street of terraced houses in Bethnal Green, crossed by an elevated railway bridge. Trains bring people in and out of Bethnal Green. **Tommy Swann** will try to escape from the police by jumping on a freight train. Now the gates of Whitechapel tube station are shut. A policeman patrols the streets. It is raining.

2. **George Sandigate** looks out of his bedroom window and sees his daughter **Vi** arriving home in a car in the early hours. He gets back into bed with his wife **Rose**.

3. At a tea stall **Whitey**, **Freddie** and **Dicey** have a cup before going off to rob a warehouse. A newspaper headline says 'Dartmoor escape'.

4. **Tommy**, a dishevelled and desperate figure, runs down a bank and reaches a railway track.

5. The street as in (1). We will return to the same location at

different times of day throughout the film.

6. **Solly Hyams** gives the newspapers that contain the news of *Tommy's* escape to the delivery boy.

7. **Rose** and **George** in bed as in (2). Rose bangs on the wall and demands a cup of tea. She is not a sympathetic character but waspish and unsmiling.

8. Rose's stepdaughters **Vi** and **Doris** in the adjoining bedroom. We have seen Vi arrive home and she tells her sister that she was drunk. She does not get on with her stepmother, although her sister Doris is more acquiescent. As Vi looks in the mirror she dreams of a world of glamour and passion, flashing back to the previous evening and her liaison with **Morry Hyams**, **Solly**'s son, record shop proprietor and dance band leader, 'The Man with Sax Appeal'. Morry seduces a willing Vi with promises of singing competitions and gifts of records.

9. The newspaper boy delivers to the tea stall in the rain as in (3). **Whitey**, **Freddie** and **Dicey** are back from robbing the warehouse but all they got was a load of children's roller skates. Now they have to get rid of them. An item on the front of the *News of the World* informs them that **Tommy Swann** has escaped prison.

10. **Detective Sergeant Fothergill** and **Detective Sergeant Leech** look for **Tommy** in a sleazy lodging house. Fothergill tells Leach about the Warehouse break-in and the stolen roller skates.

11. **Tommy Swann** has reached Bethnal Green. He hides in a church doorway before making off over a bomb site.

12. Return to **George** and **Rose**'s bedroom as in (2, 7). **Doris**

The return of Rose's repressed feelings

brings George and Rose tea and the *News of the World*. George reads out the item about **Tommy Swann**. Rose, looking in the mirror and brushing her dark hair, flashes back to her first sight of smart-suited Tommy in the mirror behind the bar at The Two Compasses where she was a blonde barmaid. She recalls their love affair. Tommy gives her a ring which ten years later he will not remember when she offers it to him to aid his escape. As Rose is packing for her departure to marry Tommy she is told that he has been arrested in a smash and grab raid. Rose returns to the present, her daily routine, haddock for breakfast and middle-aged George who is interested in darts not sex.

The different strands of the narrative are all touched by the return of Tommy except for Vi's liaison with Morry, a recent mirror image of a young blonde promised excitement and passion by a man who is not free to provide it. The other intertwining strands are no less important, as they all underline the constricting nature of Britain in the 1940s. Rose is a housewife in a lacklustre marriage who has to manage a house with few conveniences, socks that need mending and rationed food. Her stepdaughters, living at home and sharing a bed, have equally limited options: respectable Doris can keep her job as a typist at the gas works, resisting suave

Lou Hyam's attentions and settling for a tame but steady relationship with her boyfriend Ted; Vi can go to dances and have sex with a married man. She can be a 'bad girl' as Rose was and get presents but the promises that go with them are empty.

Other characters join the story, their lives woven into the everyday fabric of Bethnal Green: Morry has to convince his wife Sadie that he is not having an affair but she is too smart for him and has the measure of his roving eye; his brother Lou is surviving rationing by wheeling and dealing in the black market, also making money by fixing a boxing match; his father Solly and sister Bessie disapprove of his flashy lifestyle although Bessie wants to raise money to support a children's club; Slopey Collins, a newspaper reporter, is looking for Tommy; a woman in the market would also like to find Tommy as he left her for Rose; Doris is falling out with Ted because Lou Hyams has offered to get her a job in a beauty parlour; Rose and George's son Alfie wants a harmonica and is prepared to use a little blackmail to get it; Mr Neesley, the church organist is getting stolen goods on the cheap and the police are closing in. All of these characters have to accept, in their various ways, the world of the present. The 'dream world', the world represented in flashback in the mirror is the ephemeral past where Rose, ten years younger, was a confident blonde and caught sight of Tommy. Then he was a charming well turned-out crook and had money to throw around, now he is a dishevelled and unshaven fugitive, his back scarred by the beatings he has received in prison.

Tommy does not shatter an existing peace but a situation where there is already tension. After George has sat naked in the tin bath in the kitchen and then left to play darts in the Two Compasses Rose smuggles Tommy upstairs to her bedroom where he removes his wet clothes. The contrast between the two men is clear. As the police close in Tommy attempts to throw himself under a train but he will go back to prison and lashings from the cat. Rose tries to gas herself, not because she is ashamed but because she can see no way out. George wants her back with her family, just as Fred (although belonging to a different class in a very different film) wanted Laura back in *Brief Encounter*. Laura returns to a comfortable middle class existence, her reality the stolid if unexciting support of Fred and her well-bred children. Her dreams will be channelled into visits to the cinema and classical music on the radio. This will be a continuation of a 'decent' life, whereas in *It Always Rains on Sunday* the characters in the main are scratching around on the edges; Tommy Swann's charm was a veneer, his sexual energy was linked with violence and destruction. Threats to society are motivated by poverty but also come from constraints of energy. The law, in the shape of Jack Warner as Detective Sergeant Fothergill, can neutralise the threat that men like Tommy pose but Tommy is only the catalyst, acting to stir up the already palpable tensions and fissures within post-war society. The narrative is resolved through the suppression of emotion, and we might see here that it is the repression itself that is the real threat. Another way of dealing with Britain on the edge was to turn the situation around – to treat the sexual energy as the threat and steer the narrative towards its elimination. If society is on the edge it will be prevented from falling in by the secure arm of the law.

The Blue Lamp

Made in 1950 by the prolific producer/director/writer team of Basil Dearden and Michael Relph (the self styled 'workhorses' of Ealing) and scripted by ex-policeman T. E. B.Clarke, this was an attempt to present its audience with what was seen as a contemporary social problem.[62] A dramatic increase in recorded crime was one of the many difficulties Britain faced as it readjusted to the post-war world with a 'weakened respect for law, human life and property'.[63] This became a grave concern, and a number of films in the 1940s and 50s took crime as their focus.

Media anxieties centred on what they saw as an emerging phenomenon, the uncontrolled menace of juvenile delinquency attributed to 'an effect of a childhood spent in a home broken and ill adjusted by war' and perpetrated by dangerous young men and wayward young women. The quasi-documentary opening of the film has a commentary stating that young girls who have left home are 'all the more dangerous because of their immaturity'. The stability of the family was thus seen as being undermined by the threat of an emerging and uncontrolled sexuality in the very group that would make their voices heard in the following decade. The solution to a breakdown in national morality was, in narrative terms, to eliminate the source of the disruption and reconstitute those remaining into the wider community which would take on the responsibilities of the family. It represents one of the strands that Andrew Higson has identified at Ealing in the post-war period, a strand that we have already seen present in *It Always Rains on Sunday*:

> *those films which to some degree assume that community, that network of interrelations, as already constructed, and go on to explore the possibility – or danger – of its deconstruction by the intrusion of violent and erotic forms of individual desire... .Community is, in its most domestic form, the family. Narrative conventions of community, or family, versus individual; social responsibility versus individual desire.*[64]

The police – guardians of decency and order

If *It Always Rains on Sunday* acknowledged that passion when repressed and contained became a destructive force then *The Blue Lamp* deals with passion as a danger needing to be eliminated by the forces of moderation. Such forces are embodied in the iconic figure of P.C. 693 George Dixon, the symbol of a police force upholding the law, guardians of decency and order against the disorder of those who threaten chaos. The opening unseen Voice of God narrator asks: 'What stands between the ordinary public and the outbreak of crime? What protection has the man in the street against this armed threat against life and property?' The Voice of Established Authority, an Old Bailey judge, provides us with the answer: 'I have no doubt that one of the best preventatives of crime is the regular uniformed officer on the beat.' Set and shot in identifiable London locations – Paddington Green, Edgware Road, Ladbroke Grove, Latimer Road and White City Stadium – the film uses a social realist format to stress its base in the truth and the seriousness of its social purpose. The social realist format of *It Always Rains on Sunday* revealed that the sensual mirror world was just an illusion, its circular structure one of compromise and defeat. The narrative structure of *The Blue Lamp* is that of comforting continuity as it begins with P.C. Dixon giving directions to Paddington Green and ends with his natural successor P.C. Andy Mitchell performing the same service.

Jack Warner, already established with the audience as the figure of the law in *It Always Rains on Sunday*, is the traditional policeman loved by the community – working class, paternal, decent and upright. He and his wife have lost their only son Bert in the War but Dixon is the benevolent father figure to the community and both he and Paddington Green police will adopt Andy Mitchell as a replacement son. The Police are a family who demonstrate their solidity and male camaraderie through playing darts and singing together. Andy can move into their world because he is responsible, safe and homely. In contrast Tom Riley is a new type of criminal: young, alienated, violent and out of control. In dress and attitude Riley models himself on the gangster/outsiders of American films such as Bart Tare as played by John Dall in *Gun Crazy* (dir. Joseph H. Lewis, United Artists) released the same year. Riley is played by the already dangerous and sexually threatening young Dirk Bogarde and his image can be equated with that of the man in the 'Haunted Mirror' with the audience drawn to it and fascinated by what they feared. Andy Medhurst has described him as:

> *The underside of emotional repression, the sneer or the pout that disturbs the stiff upper lip. Bogarde in* The Blue Lamp *achieves the rare power of subversion in popular culture.*[65]

Riley is not just outside the law but also outside the criminal fraternity who make up the 'old' villains. After he has lost control and shot P.C. Dixon outside a cinema thirty-nine minutes into the film the community of criminals will co-operate with the police and help trap him and bring him to justice. They too see the need to eliminate what he stands for, a threat seen as common to them all. The restoration of order is dependent on the consensus of various groups and individuals within society. The wider community includes the

initially reluctant Queenie, an almost feral working class child whose 'Dad don't let me talk to coppers'. The narrative has moved, as John Hill notes, 'towards integration, assimilation of troubling elements

"Those who threaten chaos": the uncontrolled menace of juvenile delinquency

through appeal to good sense or reason'.[66]

The Blue Lamp was amongst the top British money-makers of 1950, winning a British Film Award for that year. It became the major image of the Police as reassuring figures not only through the film but through the stage version in 1952 and, most influentially the BBC TV series. Beginning in 1955 it brought George Dixon back from the dead to patrol Paddington (now Dock) Green for the next twenty-one years.

52 David Sharp @ http://www.screenonline.org.uk/film/id/486809/.

53 Slocombe had been a newsreel cameraman for the MOI and had covered the German invasion of Poland and Holland. George Auric had spent the war in occupied France having been a leading figure in the avant-garde of the 1920s. He became one of Ealing's house composers. He also composed the music for all Jean Cocteau's films, including *La Belle et la Bête* (1946) and *Orphée* (1950), both of which use mirrors as the gateway to another world.

54 *Monthly Film Bulletin* (14) 168: 171, December 1947.

55 Quoted in screenonline @ http://www.screenonline.org.uk/film/id/486809/, *op. cit.*

56 Scott Foundas, 'Dead Ends and Might have Beens: *It Always Rains on Sunday*', *Village Voice*, Tuesday, 4 March 2008.

57 Dilys Powell (1947) as quoted in John Ellis, 'The Discourse of Art Cinema', in *Screen* (19) 3: Autumn

1978.

58   Andrew Pulver, *The Guardian*, Friday, 5 January 2007.

59   Scott Foundas, *op. cit.*

60   George Robinson, 'British Jews, Front And Center', *The Jewish Week, New York*, 5 March 2008.

61   Charles Barr, *Ealing Studios, op.cit.*, p. 69.

62   Dearden is known for his choice of serious and socially conscious subject matter. He took the first
     tentative steps towards looking at the representation of race with *Pool of London* made at Ealing in
     1951. Later the team of Dearden and Relph were to produce key 'social problem' films for Rank:
     Sapphire (1959 Artna Films), a film about racial prejudice in the wake of the so-called Notting Hill race
     riots; and *Victim* (1961 Allied Film Makers), an appeal for the decriminalisation of homosexuality.

63   H. Mannheim (1955) *Group Problems in Crime and Punishment*, London: Routledge & Kegan Paul,
     p. 112. [Query: publisher?]

64   Andrew Higson, '"Britain's Outstanding Contribution to the Film": The Documentary-Realist Tradition',
     in Barr, *All Our Yesterdays, op. cit.*, pp. 89–90.

65   Andy Medhurst (1986) 'Dirk Bogarde', in Barr (ed.) *All Our Yesterdays, op. cit.* p.74

66   John Hill (1986) *Sex, Class and Realism: British Cinema 1956–1965*, London: BFI, p. 74.

7. EALING COMEDY 1: 'A Great Affection for British Institutions'

> In the immediate post-war years there was yet no mood
> of cynicism: the bloodless revolution of 1945 had taken
> place, but I think our first desire was to get rid of as
> many wartime restrictions as possible, and get going.
> The country was tired of regulations and regimentation
> and there was a mild anarchy in the air. In a sense our
> comedies were a reflection of this mood...a safety valve for
> our more anti-social impulses. **Michael Balcon** [67]

At any one time films can be seen to provide a disguise for
all kinds of situations and fears that concern its audiences
– about the future, different sexualities, loss of power and
erosion of a social structure. Comedy, perhaps more than any
other genre, provides a camouflage for the safe examination
of anxieties and sensitive issues which can then be diffused by
letting off steam through laughter. The material deprivations
of post-war society could be alleviated through humour and
indeed humour was often very necessary. Screenwriter T.
E. B.Clarke described the circumstances surrounding the
screening of Ealing's first new-style comedy in the winter of
1947:

> The winter was exceptionally cruel – we were being
> rationed more severely than at any time in the war. Hue
> and Cry was first shown during the coldest, grimmest,
> week of a vile February. There was virtually no heating
> at the press reception; the critics were huddled in
> overcoats and the supply of drink was unavoidably limited.
> We couldn't believe it was possible for our little effort
> to relieve the general gloom. Yet because our picture

supplied what had become another rarity – laughter – it had so joyous a welcome that it became an instant hit.[68]

The comedies for which Ealing is so famous (in spite of the fact that they comprise only a small part of their output) were made in the late 1940s and early 1950s and, like the other Ealing films, were a response to the particular post-war situation of shortages, restrictions and petty bureaucracy. In 1974 Balcon made it clear that their motivation was affection, not revolution:

If you think about Ealing at those times, we were a bundle … (I'm not saying this in any critical sense), we were middle-class people brought up with middle-class backgrounds and rather conventional educations. And although many people thought we were radical in our points of view, we were not tearing down all the institutions in our films. We did not think in terms of Marxism or Maoism, or Lévi-Strauss or Marcuse, or anything like that. We were people of the immediate post-war generation, and we voted Labour for the first time after the war; this was our mild revolution. We had great affection for British institutions; the comedies were done with affection, and I don't think we would have thought of tearing down institutions unless we had a blueprint for what we wanted to put in their place… of course we wanted… to use the cliché of today, to look for a more just society in the terms that we knew. The comedies were a mild protest, but not protests about nothing more sinister than the regimentation of the times, after a period of war. I think we were going through a mildly euphoric period then believing in ourselves and having some sense of, yes it sounds awful, national pride. And if I were to think and think I couldn't give you a deeper analysis.[69]

Ealing comedies operated, like so much of their output, on a realist basis. Watching comic fantasies about restriction was one way to handle the reality of everyday constraints.

The 'Mild Anarchy' of T. E. B. Clarke

If any one person can be credited with inventing Ealing Comedy, it would have to be T. E. B. Clarke. **Philip Kemp**[70]

Resident screenwriter Thomas Ernest Bennett 'Tibby' Clarke wrote fifteen films at Ealing between 1944 and 1957. Before that he had been a journalist producing humorous articles for the *London Evening News*. He had also worked in advertising and the police force. At Ealing his screenplays included *The Blue Lamp* and the War drama *For Those in Peril* (dir. Charles Crichton, 1944) as well as the comedies *Hue and Cry* (dir. Charles Crichton, 1947), *Passport to Pimlico* (dir. Henry Cornelius, 1949), *The Lavender Hill Mob* (dir. Charles Crichton, 1951) and *The Titfield Thunderbolt* (dir. Charles Crichton, 1953). Richard Dacre has called Clarke 'the architect of Ealing's popular image of cosy whimsicality'[71] and indeed his style is very much one we have come to come to associate with Balcon, exemplifying the philosophy of 'no point in hankering after things beyond your reach' or, as Clarke himself said: 'We didn't attempt the impossible, we attempted the just possible.' The England (for it is indeed England) depicted in the comedies is one where eccentricity is part of the national make-up and individuals take on official bureaucrats or large impersonal enterprises. The establishment was an Aunt Sally whom the comedies could throw sticks at, but not attack with any real force.

Clarke's settings are realistic and recognisable; the characters lead ordinary restricted lives. He then places them in what he called a 'what if?' situation: What if we could foil a master criminal by altering his coded messages? What if we discover that we are not really British after all? What if we steal a vanload of gold bullion and smuggle it out of the country? What if we take over a railway branch line threatened with closure? Having liberated the characters by placing them in these extraordinary situations they can proceed to indulge in their dreams and idiosyncrasies, stretching their legs in a fantasy before both narrative and social order have been restored and placed them back in the real world of conformity and control.

Hue and Cry, Clarke's first comedy for Ealing, was made in 1947. Previous comedies made by the Studio had been vehicles for performers such as George Formby and Will Hay who came to films with their personas already defined from Music Hall. *Hue and Cry* initiated the Ealing style of character performances by actors, not comedy routines by comedians, and action that takes place in realistic and recognisable settings. Shot almost entirely on location in an East London bearing the scars of the Blitz, the contemporary audience could identify with this backdrop and the subsequent fantasy of a crime/comedy/thriller could be firmly rooted in the familiar. The narrative structure also set the pattern for the Clarke/Ealing comedy. As Philip Kemp writes:

> like all Clarke's comedies ... [Hue and Cry] *celebrates a degree of anarchy – the liberating power of fantasy to break through the drab, commonsense fabric of everyday life. A group normally subject to the prosaic weight of authority (schoolboys, in this case) suddenly find themselves able to wriggle free, to realise – at least for a time – their daydreams. Yet – as so often in Clarke's work, and indeed in Ealing generally – the anarchy is limited, controlled, ultimately unambitious, feeding safely back*

into the society which surrounds and, in the end, contains it. The boys 'take over the city' for no more subversive purpose than to round up a gang of crooks.[72]

The pattern the comedies were to follow – witty script, comic performance, liberating chaos, controlled resolution – was established. In Clarke's next comedy his liberating power of fantasy was to be used as an examination of Britishness itself and its response to crisis.

Passport to Pimlico

The comedies were tremendously popular, because we'd just been through a grey period and Passport to Pimlico *was spot-on for the time. They had a streak of anarchy in them, but they were all securely rooted in the British way of life and very well written.* **Michael Relph** [73]

Passport to Pimlico (dir. Henry Cornelius, 1949) is a film which examines the idea of nationality in the wake of a conflict that had fought to defend it. We can return to Jeffrey Richard's description, quoted in the Chapter 1 of this book, of the national as 'the population that collectively occupies a defined territory'. The idea for the film was suggested by a wartime newspaper item. During the German occupation of the Netherlands the exiled Princess Juliana gave birth to her child in Ottawa, Canada in a room which was reallocated as 'Dutch' territory. That such spaces could be reassigned and a particular nationality bestowed on its occupiers is worked through in the film. In order to demonstrate an understanding of what being British is, the citizens of Miramont Place have to investigate what it is like *not* being British, except of course, the community of Miramont Place belong just as the people who live outside belong. The spirit of the nation exists in both the 'Burgundians' who hold out during the siege and the citizens of 'England' who come together and bombard them with buns. Before examining the way that the film literally sets up its own defined territory it is worth looking at extract from an article by Linda Grant, written for the *Jewish Quarterly* in 2004, which locates the source of its Englishness partly as the idealised construct of outsiders who have adopted it:

> Passport to Pimlico *is a comic investigation of Englishness. Not Britishness, which is rarely mentioned. Britain is an institutional entity, its government, Home and Foreign Office; it runs the Empire. Englishness is what the characters feel themselves to be inside... how people felt about their country in the immediate post-war years, after a struggle against both fascism abroad and the dreary restrictions of living entirely by the rule book.*

> .... *this quintessentially English film, about little England, is the hand of two strands of post-war British Jewry, the second generation shtetl immigrant, [Balcon] and the Yekke, the Central European Jewish émigré intellectual [Henry Cornelius]. 'Passport to Pimlico' is a portrait of an England idealised by immigrants.... a portrait of England from the vantage point of the grateful refugee.... Ealing studios made us an England. It exists within the small boundaries of a film released fifty-five years ago, and in the DVD playing on my laptop. This Pimlico. This little realm. This little nationality.*[74]

Her thesis examines the idea, also suggested by Jill Balcon, about the nature of people's 'roots... who are not entirely British'. If we think of some of the most 'British' examples of our national cinema – Ealing, James Carreras at Hammer Studios and Alexander Korda's London Films – these are creations of first or second generation immigrants who had particular (if not the same) ideas about what represented 'Britishness' and what such a concept meant.

In austerity Britain the audience for *Passport to Pimlico* could look back with nostalgia at the recent past and the wartime spirit. As stated peace had brought an end to fighting but not an end to shortages, and we have seen that the winters were severe. The entry into the world of the film appears to offer escape. It begins in what seems to be the tropics. A rumba is playing; a man in a white suit cooled by an electric fan looks through Venetian blinds to the heat outside. Under a parasol a man is lounging and a girl in a bathing suit is sunbathing on a rooftop – is this Havana? The camera pans downwards but it's not 'Pescado y Patatas Fritas' on offer, it's 'Fish and chips'; and the band playing on the radio is not Orlando 'Cachaito' López but Les Norman and his Bethnal Green Bambinos. We are in Britain and it's 94° on the Ministry roof. The unusual circumstances of the heat wave have created a 'foreign' atmosphere but as we come down to street level we are back in Britain. The narrative will echo this, allowing the characters to experience being foreign, but it will bring them back home to earth at its closure, which is where they want to be.

Plans for the redevelopment of the bomb site in Miramont Place, Pimlico, begin to set the story in motion and raise debates about post-war reconstruction. Arthur Pemberton, a local shopkeeper, has a scheme to develop the site as community use for local children. He wants it to become a swimming pool and playground. At a council meeting his scheme is opposed by the middle class Mr. Wix, manager of the local bank: 'We've got to face economic facts Mr Pemberton. This borough is in no position just now to finance daydreams.' The council reject the scheme in favour of selling the site for a profit. The audience are returned to the discussion that motivated them to vote in 1945: Social needs or free enterprise? Ideals or materialism? Labour or Conservative? Atlee or Churchill? Pemberton or Wix?

The narrative now needs a major plot point to really set the debate in motion. The community will be removed so that the conflicts that arise from the different arguments can be examined from a fantasy situation. Pamela, the unexploded bomb, is accidentally detonated by children playing on what they regard as their space. Pemberton accidentally falls into the resulting crater and imagines he sees a treasure. He and his daughter Shirley have indeed found a treasure, not only in the shape of coin and relics, but also ancient documents. The explosion disrupts the narrative but this is only a prelude to the major disruption that follows. At the inquest to decide will happen to the hoard we are introduced to the historian Professor Hatton-Jones, played by the arch British eccentric Margaret Rutherford. Her study of the documents explodes the second narrative bomb. The 15th century Duke of Burgundy (whose treasure this is) was not killed in battle as had been thought but was given a portion of what is now Pimlico by King Edward IV as a reward. This was never repealed; the community are really citizens of Burgundy and the booty belongs to them as Burgundians. Their debate continues, but now it is up to the community to decide how to spend the £100,000. Pemberton still wants to go forward with his scheme but Wix has not changed his views: the scheme is 'all very laudable no doubt, but where are your returns? The real benefit to the community will be some scheme for stimulating real trade and launching new enterprises.' However Wix is changing. His realisation that he need no longer be in thrall to the pompous officials from head branch leads to his to kicking over the traces enough to dance with the buoyant Mrs Randall and burn his ration book.

The film can be seen to have worked on two levels for its contemporary audience. They were experiencing restrictions that the characters in the film are able to abandon temporarily. At the same time the very recent memory of wartime sprit is something both the fictional characters and audience share: 'I'm not moving anyway. The Nazis couldn't drive me out my home with all their bombs and rockets and doodlebugs and you don't catch me packing up now.'

Whitehall, the Government, is now the enemy with its restrictions and petty laws and border controls. Yet Whitehall is Naunton Wayne and Basil Radford, lending the right air of upper class toffery to the notion that civil servants (even in the new egalitarian Socialist government) sit in comfortable offices when they are not in their stately homes, always have a biscuit (off rations) to enjoy with their tea, and wash their hands with perfumed soap stolen from the French embassy. The citizens of Miramont Place are disconnected from Whitehall's jurisdiction and connected to a Burgundy of romantic legend whose representative is Sebastien de Charolais (now able to forget the French Revolution and style himself the Duke of Burgundy). However, as he tells Shirley, in his home town of Dijon a cement factory has been built where the castle once stood. The romantic has been replaced by the prosaic. The Utopian situation will also be replaced with exploitation by outside racketeers and then with isolation. The Government closes the border, leaving the Burgundians without power, running water or their evacuated children. It is now necessary for the citizens of 'England' to come to their aid by organising a Pimlico lift of essential supplies (just as British planes were joining in the airlift of June 1948–May 1949 to 'plucky little Berlin' isolated in the now Communist East Germany). The little island of Pimlico/Burgundy can't stand alone and needs to reach a settlement. It is left to Mr

The Burgundians come home, which is where they want to be

Wix, Burgundy's Chancellor of the Exchequer, to suggest the compromise that will bring about a solution. If they loan the treasure to Britain the Burgundians can have the interest. Miramont Place can build its Lido and the citizens of Burgundy can return to Britain where their patriotism really resides. The jubilation of the community (which we could surmise suggests both the victory over the Germans and the Labour victory in the General Election) is signalled by a street party with a new ration book on every plate. As Pemberton toasts their return the rain begins and the temperature drops. We are truly back in Britain.

The post-war problems being confronted by the audience call for a return to the community spirit and co-operation of wartime. Revolution is not the answer; it is only a dream which has come to an end. What they really have reconciles them with its limitations: 'You never know when you're well off till you aren't.' Charles Barr sees the conclusion of the film as the only way to submerge 'differences that are otherwise intractable' with Wix (Tory) having to co-operate with Pemberton (Labour). He sees 'the prime fantasy of the film' not as 'the dream of release from rationing and restrictions' but a 'return to wartime solidarity, which means an intensification of rationing and restrictions: in the course of the film these become truly romanticised'.[75]

Films of course are the way of experiencing and examining fantasies and dreams, but we can return to Balcon's 'Realism or Tinsel?' speech of 1943: 'People will see that the world is rich enough and noble enough to provide for all their needs.' He saw *Passport to Pimlico* as a celebration, a rejection of a free for all economy and ethos. As Paul Wells proposes:

> *Far from being a reactionary and conservative position, this is viewed within the film as progressive because it sustains particular kinds of values and behaviour which would be lost to misdirected aspirations unsuitable to a British temperament, defined it seems, by wartime consensus and a nostalgia for imagined communities and significant nationhood.*

> *...Passport to Pimlico demonstrates and endorses the utopia of a civilised community with consensus politics sustaining the ideological status quo...a tribute to the war effort, and not merely a nostalgic longing for its terms and conditions. It is a celebration of what the British are, and what they want to be, and though it may seem conservative in its outlook to contemporary viewers, it represents a lack of cynicism which characterises the pride, dignity and hope many British people felt in the post-war period.* Passport to Pimlico *is about goodwill expressed with good humour.* [76]

Democracy or bureaucracy? One is not possible without the other. Pimlico was in no position to finance daydreams, but fortunately Ealing were.

The Lavender Hill Mob

Writing of Ealing's comedy style John Ellis has described it as belonging:

*to the type which deals with the disruption of social reality,
something that is often defined as the safe playing out
of 'base urges': the enactment of desires that are not
socially sanctioned ...dealing with the Utopian desires
of the lower middle class rather than its resentments.
Certainly resentment played a part in the working of the
comedy...but it was not its main emphasis. Rather the
style dealt with the consequences of resentment when it
was played through; the consequences were the release of
subterranean values. These values, and their laying out in
a specific area in a limited amount of time, constitute the
'fantasy'; the affectionate 'whimsicality' often noted in the
Ealing comedies.*[77]

The Lavender Hill Mob (dir.Charles Crichton, 1951) was the
second of three Ealing collaborations between Clarke and old
Etonian Charles Crichton. Scripted by Clarke the year after
The Blue Lamp the police are now part of the establishment
that the 'mob' need to outwit. Like Pimlico SW1 it is firmly
set by its title in London, in Lavender Hill, SW11, both easily
reached by public transport from Ealing W5. The normality of
the location is entered via the glamorous and foreign – like
Passport to Pimlico the film opens in Latin America, in Rio de
Janeiro, but this time we are really there. We are introduced
to Henry Holland, played by Alec Guinness who, together with
Stanley Holloway (here playing Pendlebury), were central to
the Ealing repertory company. As performers they have the
task of convincing us as spectators that they are not Guinness
and Holloway but Holland and Pendlebury, and during the
course of the film we will be confronted with their 'double
performance' – for the comedy of the film hinges on the
difference between what things *appear* to be and what they
really are.

Mild Henry Holland, transformed by crime

So the bar is in exotic sunny Rio de Janeiro (although it really is on one of the sound stages at Ealing). Suave, assured Henry Holland is living the dream of escape from cold drab austerity England. He begins to tell his story. In London, one year earlier, Holland, then a meticulous bank clerk who appears to be unimaginative, is responsible for supervising deliveries of gold bullion from the refinery to the Bank of England. He is one of a crowd who go about their daily routine in the London streets, and this anonymity will later allow him to mingle with the throng and escape the police. This is the outer world of post-war England, its rationing and restrictions not part of the camaraderie of Miramont Pace but the 'millions' who lead humdrum lives. The world Holland inhabits appears to be overwhelming him with its instructions – 'Wipe your feet', 'Switch off the light'. He speaks of the 'dream' of millions; his fantasy is to commit the perfect robbery. This is a harmless daydream, a 'mild protest' – a gesture of defiance against conformity, an echo of a crime novel taking place in his head. At his lodgings at the Balmoral Private Hotel in Lavender Hill he reads such novels to Mrs Chalk, his seemingly prim fellow tenant, who enters wholeheartedly into the spirit of *You'd Look Good in a Shroud*. These are escapist stories where Duke Milligan is about to take a gander at Mickey the Greek's hideout in a world far removed from the Balmoral Hotel, but behind his mild exterior Holland is plotting to commit the perfect crime. To do this he needs a partner. Pendlebury arrives as the new tenant with all the panache and the equipment of an artist, but in reality he is an amateur whose art is 'his wings, his escape' and whose main occupation is casting cheap souvenirs in metal. Pendlebury's tourist memorabilia includes Eiffel Tower paperweights for export to Paris, painted gold to make them appear more expensive. Holland suggests the gold could be smuggled to France in the form of what *appear* to be solid lead paperweights.

Cops and Robbers

The two would-be criminals are contrasting characters: Pendlebury is boisterous, much more verbose and quotes freely from Shakespeare; Holland, described by his superiors as a 'nonentity', is meek, retiring, seemingly cautious and softly spoken. Both appear to be 'honest men' but are plotting to become Dutch and Al, Master Criminals who need a gang. They attract two Cockney professional petty thieves, Lackery Wood and Shorty Fletcher, by setting up a trap that appears to be a genuine conversation.

The robbery goes almost to plan apart from Pendlebury being wrongfully arrested on suspicion of stealing a painting from a street stall. As an alibi, Shorty and Lackery bind and blindfold Holland so that he will appear to have been attacked. Pendlebury's assistant runs a kiosk at the top of the Eiffel Tower. Due to a language misunderstanding, however, she has mistakenly sold six of the solid gold Towers to a party of English schoolgirls. Holland and Pendlebury visit the girls' school in Hendon, where they appear to be concerned as they attempt to exchange five lead statues for gold ones. One little girl, however, refuses to swap and they follow her to a police open day where 'real' police are mixed with 'historical' police and 'dummy' police. Mayhem ensues as Holland and Pendlebury steal a police radio car and pretend to be policeman. The hilarious car chase through London streets (where the Force's radio antennae becomes entwined with that of an ordinary car and ends up broadcasting 'Old MacDonald had a Farm' over the police radio) underlines the affectionate parody of *The Blue Lamp*.

The narrative restores order and normality; the fantasy is taken away. Holland who appeared to be enjoying the freedom of Rio is in reality in handcuffs. The million pounds is beyond his reach; the criminals are eccentric but harmless. We might consider though that it was the compensating values demanded by the Censors of the early 1950s that appear to be imposing a resolution of 'crime does not pay'. In fact crime transforms Holland into the confident worldly man we saw at the beginning of the film. His 'subterranean values' have been released and no one has been hurt (although the last we saw of Pendlebury was in the hands of the law). Philip Kemp suggests:

> *Of all the Clarke comedies,* The Lavender Hill Mob *comes closest to shattering these self-prescribed limits. Alec Guinness's downtrodden, patronized bank clerk does get away with his stolen bullion, does enjoy the high life in South America – but even here convention imposes, in the last reel, a well-spoken Interpol detective, complete with handcuffs.*[78]

It would be nice to think that Holland only *appears* to be under arrest. In 'reality' he got away with it.

67 Michael Balcon, *A Lifetime of Films, op. cit.*, p. 159.

68 As quoted in Charles Barr, *Ealing Studios, op. cit.*, p. 94.

69 Michael Balcon (1975) in an interview with John Ellis, *op.cit.*, p. 119.

70 Philip Kemp @ http://www.filmreference.com/Writers-and-Production-Artists-Ch-De/
    Clarke-T-E-B.html.

71 Richard Dacre (1997)'Traditions of British Comedy', in Robert Murphy (ed.) *The British Cinema Book*,
    London: BFI, p. 236.

72 Philip Kemp@ http://www.filmreference.com/Writers-and-Production-Artists-Ch-De/
    Clarke-T-E-B.html , *op. cit.*

73 Michael Relph (1993) as interviewed by Robin Buss, 'England's Dreaming', *op. cit.* [Query: page
    numbers?]

74 Linda Grant, 'This Little Realm', *Jewish Quarterly* 195: Autumn 2004. [Query: page numbers?]

75 Charles Barr, *Ealing Studios, op. cit.*, pp. 103–4.

76 Paul Wells @ http://www.filmreference.com/Films-Or-Pi/Passport-to-Pimlico.html.

77 John Ellis, 'Made in Ealing', *op. cit.*, p. 114.

78 Philip Kemp @ http://www.filmreference.com/Writers-and-Production-Artists-Ch-De/
    Clarke-T-E-B.html, *op. cit.*

8. EALING COMEDY 2: 'A Piece of Poisoned Chocolate in a Beautifully Wrapped Box' [78]

> *Hamer and Mackendrick belonged to Ealing: it trusted them and forms the context within and against which their individuality defines itself. Their work both contributes to and comments on Ealing and its values, and we need to see them in continuous relation to this context*
>
> **Charles Barr** [79]

There is another side of Ealing, one that is represented by the films of Robert Hamer and Alexander Mackendrick, who were both able to push against the parameters provided by the secure boundaries of the Studio. This is particularly evident in the black comedies which use violence and murder to form what has been called a subversive commentary on Ealing's (and Britain's) values. *Kind Hearts and Coronets* (dir. Robert Hamer, 1949) is the opposite of cosy and complacent, it is aloof and unprincipled, whereas *The Ladykillers* (dir. Alexander Mackendrick, 1955) presents us with the relics and traditions of 'old Britain' but without the reverence.

Kind Hearts and Coronets

When first presented with the idea for *Kind Hearts and Coronets* Balcon is reputed to have said: 'I'm not going to make a comedy about eight murders!' and had to be persuaded by Ealing's top creative personnel to sanction what is often regarded as one of British cinema's finest achievements. John Landis finds it:

> *Outrageous – its wit and its elegance and just how outrageous it is. It is dealing with murder and sex. It's like Titus Andronicus – bodies falling all over the place.* [80]

Balcon thought Hamer 'one of the most remarkable of the young men I gathered round me at Ealing' although he was also 'engaged on a process of self destruction'.[81] His previous films as we have seen had also depicted eruptions of sex and violence as disturbances in the narrative. From a cultured middle class family background he had been a Cambridge undergraduate but failed to take his mathematics degree because of a scandal involving an affair with a man. Much has been written about the attitude to homosexuality in the years before the 1960s when it ceased to be a criminal offence. Gay men had to repress their desires or risk breaking the law. Hamer knew all about repression.

He had started his career as an assistant in the cutting room for Gaumont-British and then worked with European film-makers at Denham. He joined the GPO film Unit and when Cavalcanti moved to Ealing he recruited Hamer as a film editor. *Kind Hearts and Coronets*, his fourth film assignment for Ealing, is the only period piece among the comedies. Set in 1902 this immediately provides the distance from which it can examine Britishness – not as community, camaraderie or consensus but as individual desire, selfishness and privilege. Its mannered style and artificiality go against the 'reality' of *Passport to Pimlico* which was being filmed on Ealing's sound stages at the same time. This apparently necessitated relocating the interior shots of *Kind Hearts* to Rank's studios at Pinewood, which were larger and had a technically superior lighting system. The distance between the two comedies was far more than the eighteen miles between London W5 and Pinewood, Buckinghamshire. If *Passport* works through the need to reconcile individual differences in order to allow the community to function happily, *Kind Hearts* provides a picture of 'there's no such thing as community' in a Britain where inheritance, snobbery and the stifling hand of tradition are almost insuperable barriers to both individual pleasure and material progress. *Passport* provides its audience with familiar surroundings and familiar, if fanciful, situations; to be British is to be resilient, to take on the bureaucrats and win through with often stoic resolve. *Kind Hearts* needed to detach them from the present and expected in order to examine the repressions that were imposed on them: Britishness is equated with snobbery; to be stoic is to be able to commit murders whilst keeping a straight face.

The artificiality of the *mise-en-scène* is perfectly matched by the artificiality of the dialogue; its upper class comedy of manners reflected in its structure and use of language. Hamer had clearly stated his aim when writing the screenplay:

> *Firstly that of making a film not noticeably similar to any previously made in the English language. Secondly that of using the English language, which I love, in a more varied and, to me, more interesting way than I had previously had the chance of doing in a film. Thirdly that of making a picture which paid no regard whatever to established, although not practised, moral convention, in which a whole family is picked off by a mass murderer.*[82]

Both the language and the moral tone stem from the original novel on which the film was based. *Israel Rank: the Autobiography of a Criminal* was written in 1902 by Roy Horniman, a follower of Oscar Wilde. Israel tells his story as first person narrator:

> *There is an old saying, 'Murder will out.' I am really unable to see why this should be so. I am convinced that many a delightful member of society has found it necessary at some time or other to remove a human obstacle, and has done so undetected and undisturbed by those pangs of conscience which Society, afraid of itself, would have us*

believe wait upon the sinner.[83]

Hamer's screenplay alludes to great writers of the English language – Chaucer, Shakespeare, Longfellow and Tennyson. The title is a quotation from Tennyson's 1842 poem *Lady Clara Vere de Vere* which proclaims that 'Kind hearts are more than coronets, and simple faith than Norman blood' although there are not many kind hearts or much simple faith in this film.

The period setting, the language, the moral tone, the casting of Alec Guinness (who keeps reappearing as all the murder victims: 'Why play four parts? Why not eight?'), these all contribute to the distancing effect. Whereas the T. E. B. Clarke comedies allow the spectator to indulge in harmless fantasies through daydreams where they can visit their desires and momentarily indulge in them, *Kind Hearts* places the spectator in the necessary position of keeping a distance from such desires because they are so base that they cannot possibly acknowledge them. This distancing, this *necessary* artificiality must be the reason why the director and critic Lindsay Anderson singled out the film in 1964 as an example of the barrenness of British cinema and Ealing comedies, describing it as 'emotionally quite frozen'.[84] The apparently frozen nature of the film is, however, as Louis d'Ascoyne himself, a surface covering a mass of tensions and emotions that centre on patriarchy, snobbery, culture and inheritance, a radical criticism of the British class system and British hypocrisy. The half Jewish Israel Rank of the novel becomes the half Italian Louis Mazzini who narrates his story in flashback. Played by Dennis Price as the embodiment of the upper class Englishman he is detached, cool, totally unflustered. He could be an officer on the bridge of a British destroyer at the beginning of the War. Louis, however, has two sides, his face a mask as he plots to murder eight of his relatives. His mother was an unemotional English aristocrat, his father a flamboyant Italian opera singer.

Louis, driven by personal desire with no debate about community or social responsibility

As he sits in his prison cell awaiting execution for murder Louis is writing his memoirs. What we are *hearing* is the unspontaneous *written* word with all the formality of its copperplate handwriting and meticulous verbal use of grammar and punctuation. Cameraman Douglas Slocombe thought Hamer was almost a stage director – he just wanted to tell the story in sound terms:

> His approach on the floor was to almost ignore the camera, he wasn't interested in set up, lighting or camera movement.[85]

The voice constructs the meaning of the visual image but can also sometimes oppose it. Louis' commentary prepares us for what we are about to witness, remarks on things that we are watching or makes observations on things that have happened. The two levels – calm politeness on the outside and murderous hatred on the inside – create a conflict between sound and image, the characters are oblivious to what Louis is thinking but the spectator is not. The nature of the medium tends to favour the veracity of what we see, and therefore 'know'. We are accustomed to measuring the photographed 'truth' by believing what we have witnessed with our eyes. In a film it may be the case that a character says he is thinking something or denies something that we have seen happen, but we usually believe what the camera has told us. In *Kind Hearts and Coronets* we see:

- A film set in the Edwardian era, the characters wearing formal and elegant costumes have formal and elegant manners.

- A man of taste and exemplary conduct whose feelings are all under control.

At the same time we hear:

- Louis' voice over contradicting his external behaviour and telling us of his inner desire to murder his victims. The precise language itself contradicts the violence of the thoughts it expresses:

  I made an oath that I would revenge the wrongs her family had done her. It was no more than a piece of youthful bravado, but it was one of those acorns from which great oaks are destined to grow. Even then I went so far as to examine the family tree and prune it to just the living members. But what could I do to hurt them? What could I take from them, except, perhaps, their lives?

We know:

- That the veneer of politeness is a sham and Louis is carrying out his plan in order to gain his revenge and move into the upper class.

Class distinctions are everywhere: in the rituals of the prison, in Louis' visit to Chalfont as a tourist, in his treatment as a draper's assistant, in the hotel at Maidenhead. At the opening of the film the hangman, played by Miles Malleson, arrives at the prison to hang Louis, now tenth Duke of Chalfont, in the morning. Louis' icy calm exhibits the kind of *sang froid* that

"Some of them tend to be very hysterical – so inconsiderate"

will make the hangman's job so much easier: 'A difficult client can make things most distressing. Some of them tend to be very hysterical. So inconsiderate.' He is concerned about how one addresses a Duke, but is grateful for the privilege such an act will bestow on him: 'I intend to retire. After using the silken rope I will never again be content with hemp.' Such obsequiousness as he prepares to murder a member of the aristocracy contrasts with Louis' own assertive executions, all performed with verbal panache mostly off camera.

Louis' actions are driven by an individual personal desire – there is no debate about community or social responsibility. His revenge centres on the d'Ascoynes for their callous treatment of his mother but broadens out to the British aristocracy that excluded them from their ranks, and the family for their stifling and rigid structure. As Philip Kemp writes:

> *Hamer's instincts drew him toward dramatic confrontation, the irreconcilable clash of motives and emotions.* Kind Hearts and Coronets, *his most accomplished film, not only traces the working out of a ruthless program of personal vengeance but mounts a sustained attack on conventional morality and the institution of the family, both of which he had cause to detest.*[86]

The confrontations were not only present inside the film. The violence of the murders is set against the strong sexual theme. Louis is faced with a choice between two women: Edith (played by the elegant Valerie Hobson), who is aristocratic and frigid; and Sibella (the provocative Joan Greenwood), upper middle class, passionate but who is prepared to settle for the more successful, if sexually inadequate, Lionel Holland. Hamer found the sexual conflict central to the morality of the film. This led to a clash with Balcon who was alarmed by the erotic aspects of the contrast between Sibella and Edith and wanted their difference to be those of class. Hamer refused to give way which resulted in a very public row. Balcon's well documented attitude to sex accounted for its rare appearance in an Ealing film. Bryan Forbes' remark that 'sex was buried with full military honours at Ealing'[87] is borne out by Charles Crichton's observation about Balcon that:

> *Sex was a big problem. I do think he knew how babies*
> *were born but it was not a subject we were allowed to treat*
> *on the screen.*[88]

The fact is that, just as the violence mainly happens off screen, the eroticism of the film lies mainly in the language. What is inferred whilst the characters are tightly buttoned into their restricting costumes is part of the surface/underneath, said/not said aspect of the film. Another example of inference is the film's deliciously ambiguous ending. As with *The Lavender Hill Mob* censorship (particularly for the film's American release where they demanded more conclusive punishment) required that though the audience might get pleasure from watching crimes committed on screen they had to be reminded that perpetrators of crime would meet their just desserts in the final reel. Louis, awaiting execution for the murder of Lionel, Sibella's husband (one crime he did not commit), has written his memoirs about the ones that he did. Released from prison through the revealing of Lionel's suicide note he realises that the incriminating evidence is still sitting on the table in his cell. The camera closes in on the book, the narration of the film. The inference that this will provide the law with the evidence to finally hang Louis is there for the censorship board, but equally it is possible that the memoires of the tenth Duke of Chalfont were retrieved and destroyed, and their contents can remain forever for our delight as secret revelations inside Louis' head.

The Ladykillers

> Mick glanced at Sandy. "Is it he who has lost his mind or have you both lost your minds? Just let me get this straight. You have six principle actors and at the end of the film five of them are dead – and you say this is a comedy?"
> **William Rose**[89]

Alexander Mackendrick was born in the USA and educated in Scotland. He joined the Studio in 1946 as a screenwriter and made seven films there as director including four comedies: *Whisky Galore!* (1949), *The Man in the White Suit* (1951), *The Maggie* (1954) and *The Ladykillers*. He then went to Hollywood, where his first film was *Sweet Smell of Success* (1957). For Mackendrick comedy was a way of circumnavigating both censorship and traditional attitudes:

> Personally I was always very attracted by comedy, at least a certain form of comedy, because I think there are things which comedy alone can say. It allows you to make things happen that are too dangerous or that a certain public cannot (otherwise) accept.[90]

Whisky Galore! is unusual for an Ealing film because even the interiors were shot on location. It pokes sly fun at Britain's most powerful ally in its assertion that 'to the West there is nothing – except America' and also at English 'colonisation' within a 'united' kingdom. The English man Waggett is the only puritanical character, undermined by the Scottish islanders. As described by Darrah O'Donoghue the film is also:

> ...a characteristic study of emasculation. Whisky Galore! depicts a world where the 'real' men have gone off to fight in the war, leaving behind simple, infirm, elderly or emotionally feeble males. It is strange that in wartime there are so few women on the island, as if it is they who have gone off to fight, leaving behind a 'feminised' patriarchy.[91]

The Man in the White Suit is a study and caricature of political attitudes as well as personal ones. Its theme of refusal to adapt to a changing world can be read as a criticism of both British and Ealing values. According to Mackendrick all the characters were based on Ealing personalities. The character of Birnley, the benevolent, paternal autocratic mill owner who tries to suppress the invention of a young idealistic employee, was an in-joke highly recognisable to the Ealing fraternity, with Birnley using some of Balcon's actual lines. Emasculated men and change thwarted by tradition are both themes that come together in The Ladykillers. This was the last comedy made at Ealing and also Mackendrick's last film for the studio where, to quote Philip Kemp, he used 'the ossified weight of the Ealing tradition against itself'.[92]

By 1955 political attitudes had changed. The Conservatives had been elected in 1951 just as austerity came to an end. They were led by Winston Churchill who, as wartime Prime Minister, had been the 'voice of Britain' broadcast to the world. Their General Election Manifesto stated:

We must guard the British way of life, hallowed by centuries of tradition. We have fought tyrants at home and abroad to win and preserve the institutions of constitutional Monarchy and Parliamentary government. From Britain across the generations our message has gone forth to all parts of the globe.

The new Government were able to use rising productivity and full employment to end rationing and restrictions and bring in a new era of consumerism and affluence. This period of growth coincided with, and probably partly caused, a period of decline in the cinema. The British film industry had been revitalised by the War when its audiences had both responded and contributed to its messages. As Britain moved into a new, more prosperous, age the social changes germinated during the War were beginning to emerge and spectators reflected these changes. By the mid to late 1950s attitudes were changing but the films were not. British cinema, hampered by its middle class way of thinking, was not secure or free enough to break with convention. It continued to look backward to the 'centuries of tradition' and 'guard the British way of life'. For those frustrated by what they saw as social and cultural stagnation Britain was a country ruled by complacent, out-of-touch cliques where power was in the hands of the old establishment.

The Ladykillers portrays such a country. Like *Kind Hearts* it is a black comedy, a displacement of unease into an absurd scenario which allows it to be safely contemplated as a fable. Mackendrick described it as:

obviously a parody of Britain in its subsidence. That we were all aware of at a certain level. But it was never openly discussed, and it would have been fatal to discuss it.[93]

Such a parodic form needed careful treatment:

> *I knew that I was trying to work on a fable. The characters are all caricatures... none of them is real for a moment... it's very dangerous when you try to combine the fantastic (like Alec's performance which I think is a marvellous caricature figure) if you post that against an actuality. You have to keep within the enclosed, fabulous world.*[94]

The enclosed fabulous world of the little house in the cul-de-sac is literally a dream one. William Rose, the American screenwriter 'woke up one morning...wakened my wife and said "I've just dreamt a whole film". I kept pushing over the origin, it wasn't like any idea I'd ever had. It was whole and complex and it was original.'[95] Mackendrick saw dreams 'as a marvellous source of imagery for movies'.

In T. E. B.Clarke's 'daydream' scenarios characters push against conventions but no one gets hurt. Sources of disruption are assimilated or contained by the narrative and order is restored. In *The Ladykillers* the sources of disruption are eliminated one by one, with equal violence, so that the equilibrium of Mrs Wilberforce's world can continue undisturbed. Alec Guinness plays a mild dreamer in *The Lavender Hill Mob*, a bank clerk whom no one would suspect to be plotting crime. In *The Ladykillers* Guinness is a sinister Gothic figure who lives up to his macabre image by posing as the bogus Professor Marcus and leading a gang of diverse individuals. The humour of the narrative hides what Mackendrick states as something deadly serious: .

> *I only laugh at things that have got some undercurrent of something deadly serious. To be frivolous about frivolous matters, that's merely boring. To be frivolous about something that's in some way deadly serious, that's true comedy.*[96]

The film is set not in the past, but in the present which continually looks to the past, the world where Victorian values linger on in profusion, signified by the setting, the house, Mrs Wilberforce and her friends.

The setting of St Pancras Station and the Station Hotel are both prime examples of the Victorian High Gothic Style and monuments to Victorian capitalism, built to receive the

Mrs Wilberforce's wonky house, at the dead end of the street

steam trains now being phased out, and running on the Nationalised railways. The house, at the end of a dead end and devoid of modern conveniences, has sustained bomb damage during the War which has caused it to subside and nothing hangs straight. Constructed in a real cul-de-sac by art director Jim Morahan and shot by cinematographer Otto Heller with the massive camera necessary for the three-strip Technicolor system, it was difficult to move through the house's wonky spaces cluttered with Victorian bric-a-brac.

Mrs Wilberforce is introduced by a tinkling musical box playing a Victorian drawing-room ballad *The Last Rose of Summer*. She could also be thought of subsiding and in her apparent absent mindedness to be slightly wonky. (One Round affectionately calls her 'Mrs Lopsided'.) Katie Johnson plays her with all the apparent quaintness and eccentricity covering the imperious confidence of the middle class elderly woman. She steadfastly maintains values and decorum at all times, instilled in her by the woman she can still recall who had headed the State and the Empire. As she celebrated her twenty-first birthday in Pangbourne she 'heard that the old Queen had passed away'. Her parrots and cockatoo commemorate Britain as a world power, named after General Gordon (Victoria's favourite general) and Admiral of the Fleet Beatty. Her costume, hairstyle, manners are all those of the bygone age. They suggest a sweet old lady but she is not a (grand)motherly figure and one assumes that she and the late Captain Wilberforce were childless. She stops on the steps of the police station to look at a baby in a pram, but the sight of her causes the baby to howl. Mrs Wilberforce will stand no nonsense. Her reaction to the revelation that the members of the string quintet are really robbers using classical music to cover their plotting is to be 'shocked and appalled'. She chastises hardened criminals like naughty schoolboys 'simply try for one hour to behave like gentlemen'. Her friends, genteel dotty old ladies with old fashioned names such as Lettice and Hypatia, are equally old fashioned in their dress and manners. They gather round Professor Marcus at the pianola to sing *Silver Threads among the Gold*, a distortion of the power of singing to unify the group that we have seen in films such as *San Demetrio, London* and *The Blue Lamp*. Here members of London's underworld are emasculated, left awkwardly balancing bone china cups of tea in a cluttered Victorian drawing room.

The area around King's Cross has the feel of a village community, suggested by the greetings Mrs Wilberforce receives as she makes her way along the street to the police station. She is well known by the kindly local police, amiably tolerated and humoured. The sergeant is played by Jack Warner, soon to be reincarnated as the benevolent Sergeant Dixon of Dock Green (Mackendrick had acted as second unit director on *The Blue Lamp*). Mrs Wilberforce has come with the news that her friend Amelia, who had reported seeing a space ship (a common theme of the 1950s) hasn't seen it again: 'She never saw it in the first place. The whole thing was just a dream.'

At the station her conversation with the Sergeant is of duty and nostalgia. It was her 'duty to come here and explain'. Nostalgia is for the old days: 'I can't think why they would want to come. We seem so overcrowded. It was so different when I was a girl.'

From peaceful benign settings we now move into horror territory. As Mrs Wilberforce leaves the station she moves into shadow. There is a clap of thunder; a black car like a hearse passes in the background. Prime Minister Winston Churchill's image, drawn by a pavement artist, starts to get wet. Sinister music plays as she enquires in the newsagents about her advertisement for the room she has to rent. We are introduced to Professor Marcus as a shadow in a homburg hat, recalling

the first appearance of M, the child murderer in Fritz Lang's 1931 German film of the same name (Mackendrick was a great admirer of Lang's

"Simply try for one hour to behave like gentlemen"

work). Professor Marcus appears a cousin of Rottwang, the mad scientist in Lang's *Metropolis* (1925) although Guinness said that he had in mind the Wolf from Red Riding Hood (about to swallow Grandma, which was the beginning of his undoing).

The Gang are figures from the more recent cinematic past.

'Major' Courtney (Cecil Parker, the Birnley/Balcon from *The Man in the White Suit*), an impersonator of the upper ranks from a British war film, but unable to kill; Louis (Herbert Lom), the sinister foreigner who, with the dim-witted lumpen proletariat One Round (Danny Green, an ex-boxer) are characters from a shady *noir* crime drama, and Harry (Peter Sellers) in his Teddy boy suit represents the new generation who hang around street corners in a social problem film. The performances of the central characters are the key, 'no one in the film tries to be funny'.

Mackendrick's comedy may be similar to Hamer's in its deposal of characters for our amusement but they are very different in their approach to the material. Louis d'Ascoyne is well aware of everything that is going on and can adapt decisively to situations – if he can't eliminate a d'Ascoyne by administering poison he'll set the boat in which his victim is dallying adrift and drown him; and if this fate is shared by a girl with whom he has no quarrel, Louis finds a witty way to justify it. Mackendrick manipulates his characters by placing them in situations of which they are either oblivious (Mrs Wilberforce) or indecisive (the Gang). Hamer, both director and screenwriter, placed great emphasis on the dialogue; Mackendrick always thought in terms of images which for him 'communicate faster than words .... at their best when they come as explanations or development of images'.[97] Another marked difference is Mackendrick's complete absence of sexuality or family in a community of eccentric old ladies and benevolent policemen.

The plot has a simple symmetry. The Gang plan their crime, use an old lady as unwitting courier and steal the money. She finds out about the crime, they plan to eliminate her, but kill each other. Mrs Wilberforce returns to the police station. The story she recounts of gangs, robbers and stolen 'lolly' has echoes of the aliens that her friend Amelia saw: 'They all disappeared during the night. You're not suggesting I imagined all this?' She is left to keep all the money. As she leaves she forgets her umbrella just as she did in the opening sequence. We are left with *The Last Rose of Summer* and the high angle shot of the house. Nothing has changed, Mrs Wilberforce has learned nothing, and England is as before. Richards and Aldgate suggest that the film echoed the stagnation of Britain in the 1950s (they call their chapter on the film 'Cul-de-Sac England') and end their analysis with the observation that:

> there is no evidence to suggest that the critics who reviewed it saw it as a critique of England. ...This suggests that the film was seen as being squarely in the mainstream, whimsical Ealing tradition. If the cinema-going public reacted in the same way, it seems likely that it took what Mackendrick intended as a satire on the Ealing view of England as a celebration of that view. They identified, in other words, with the old lady and not with the exasperated and frustrated gang who are her victims. Mrs Wilberforce's world is an apt metaphor for mid 1950s England, a cul-de-sac slumbering peacefully but shortly to be violently awakened.[98]

Change thwarted by tradition, emasculated men? Philip Kemp suggests that the notion of Ealing films as cosy is 'not an accusation that can plausibly be levelled at Mackendrick'.[99] He goes on to describe some of Mackendrick's output as his 'Condition of England' films:

> Taken together, they portray a stagnant, inhibited country, at once complacent and resentful, soured by snobbery and class conflict, hamstrung by deference to authority – petrified, in every sense in the face of change.

The Ladykillers is a film that we might see as demonstrating these qualities. It shares its 'black' tone with that of *Kind Hearts* and stands at the opposite end of the spectrum to the T. E. B.Clarke 'what if?' comedies such as *The Lavender Hill Mob*. Clarke's comedies release the characters' subterranean values by letting them commit crimes but then rounding them up and containing them in the final reel. *Kind Hearts* shows the Edwardian heir of Victorian snobbery and class division able to commit the ultimate crime of mass murder and dispatch the aristocracy that stand in his way; *The Ladykillers* shows the Edwardian heir to Victorian middle class values carrying these on into the 1950s, thwarting the attempts of the criminals trying to dispatch her.

78   John Landis (2000) description of *Kind Hearts and Coronets*, interviewed in *Forever Ealing, op. cit.*

79   Charles Barr, *Ealing Studios, op. cit.*, p. 48.

80   John Landis interviewed in *Forever Ealing, op. cit.*

81   Michael Balcon, *A Lifetime of Films, op. cit.*, pp. 162–3.

82   Robert Hamer as quoted in Barr, *Ealing Studios, op. cit.*, p. 122.

83   Roy Horniman (1902) *Israel Rank* first published by Chatto and Windus in 1907, reprinted in 1946 and published by Eyre and Spottiswoode.

84   Lindsay Anderson 'Kind Hearts and Coronets' in *Films and Filming* (10) 7: April 1964. Anderson was commenting on Hamer's depiction of the British class system at a time when British social realist films such as *Room at the Top* (Jack Clayton, 1959 Remus).and *Saturday Night and Sunday Morning* (Karel Reisz, 1960 Woodfall Film Productions) had spearheaded the British New Wave. In 1968 Anderson's own film *If* was to use extreme violence as his own radical criticism of the British class system.

85   Douglas Slocombe (1986) interviewed in *Omnibus Made in Ealing, op. cit.*

86   Philip Kemp, 'Kind Hearts and Coronets: Ealing's Shadow Side', Criterion Collection Essay, 21 February 2006 @ http://www.criterion.com/current/posts/414.

87 Bryan Forbes (1974) *Evening Standard* review of Alexander Walker's *Hollywood England* quoted in Ellis, *Made in Ealing*, op. cit., p. 123.

88 Charles Crichton (1986) interviewed in *Omnibus: Made in Ealing, op. cit.*

89 William Rose (1986) *Omnibus: 'Made in Ealing'*, op. cit.

90 Alexander Mackendrick *Positif* , 92 February 1968, p. 41 as quoted in Aldgate and Richards (1983) Best of *British: Cinema and Society 1930–1970*, Oxford: Blackwell, p. 105.

91 Darrah O'Donoghue, *Senses of Cinema*, March 2005 @ http://archive.sensesofcinema.com/contents/cteq/05/35/whisky_galore.html.

92 Philip Kemp (1991) *Lethal Innocence: The Cinema of Alexander Mackendrick*, London: Methuen, p. 111.

93 Mackendrick as quoted in Kemp, *Lethal Innocence, op. cit.*, p. 110.

94 *Ibid.*

95 William Rose (1986) in *Omnibus: Made in Ealing, op. cit.*

96 Alexander Mackendrick in Kemp, *op. cit.*

97 Alexander Mackendrick (1986), in *Made in Ealing, op. cit.*

98 Richards and Aldgate (1983) *Best of British: Cinema and Society 1930–1970*, Oxford: Blackwell, p.113.

99 Philip Kemp, *Lethal Innocence, op. cit.*, p. 73.

9. BRITISH 50S CINEMA: Changing National Values

The 'Britain of the Radical Middle Classes'[100]

1951, the year of the Festival of Britain,... was a turning point for the film industry in general: the 'X' certificate was introduced in a attempt to stem the decline in cinema audiences by moving into sensational and previously forbidden areas of sex and violence, under pressure on the one hand from the influx of 'Continental' sex films and European art cinema, and on the other from competition for audiences from television.

.....it does seem that 1951 can be seen as a pivotal year for British society, marking a shift from a period of post-war austerity, presided over by a Labour government dedicated to welfare capitalism, to the consumer boom of the 1950s managed by a new tough breed of Conservatives. The shift can also be characterised in terms of changing national values, community spirit giving way to individual and an increasing emphasis on the private domain of home and family. Culturally, the British dedication to high art values of 'quality', 'taste' and 'realism' was to be assaulted by the influx of American consumer goods and popular culture, scandalising intellectuals from both left and right.

Pam Cook[101]

At the beginning of the 1950s television began to succeed radio as the major form of communication with the BBC as the sole broadcaster. At first TV continued the same middle class, family programming, conveying the same traditional values, but, by the end of the decade these values were beginning to be questioned. In the Ealing films of the 1950s traditional values were reflected in the more serious dramas as well as the comedies. *Mandy* (dir. Alexander Mackendrick), released in

1952 and *The Cruel Sea* (dir. Charles Frend), released the year after, both embody and examine contemporary gender issues within a middle class framework: *Mandy*, a melodrama with a domestic setting and central female protagonists, and *The Cruel Sea*, a re-examination of national values, revisiting the War but now as a masculine province, solely concerned with male relationships and male emotions.

Mandy

> *Sex roles, of course, are among the most rigid of these prescribed categories; and though it would be absurd to claim Mandy as a consciously feminist work 'avant la lettre', its conclusion can be read as an almost textbook example of a woman's achievement being appropriated, defused and absorbed by a patriarchal structure.*
>
> **Philip Kemp**[102]

As far as women were concerned the 1950s were often a time of frustration. The War had provided them with an independence they had not experienced before; by 1943 every woman under 40 was expected to work and even women with young children had been conscripted into employment. They had worked alongside or in place of men (although not receiving equal pay), and experienced more sexual freedom. The Beveridge Report had stressed the importance of their post-war role and the part they would have to play in the construction of a New Britain. After the War the men returned to take up their former positions and women were expected to settle back into their previous domestic and maternal roles – but the domestic scene was changing. By the late 1940s and early 1950s the falling birth-rate allowed women to be freer and more active in the labour force, encouraged by a labour shortage as Britain sought to rebuild its industry. New consumer goods not only became available but desirable, promoted by advertising aimed at women and also by the Hollywood films which depicted a lifestyle where such goods were ostentatiously displayed. The expectation of rising living standards included the acquisition of appliances that would cut down on the time it took to do household chores, initiating the circle of having more free time which could be spent in going out to work to earn the money to buy the goods.[103] Women were therefore important as consumers but this was part of, and had to complement, their principal role as housewives and mothers. The mother's primary concern was for the welfare and emotional stability of her child, maternal deprivation was seen to be the cause of juvenile delinquency. In films such as *The Blue Lamp* it was the War that had been blamed but now the blame seemed to be shifting to working or absent mothers – by 1958 *Violent Playground* (dir. Basil Dearden, Rank Organisation) could locate the solution to the problem of delinquent youth as 'a little bit of dad and a lot of mum'. Pam Cook has proposed this period as one of shift and transition with a:

> *proliferation of competing ideologies, testifying to national uncertainty about traditional values and their effectiveness in the post-war Britain of new technologies, egalitarian social democracy, and sexual emancipation.*

She describes *Mandy* as:

> *an attempt by Ealing to negotiate a shifting terrain at a time when its future was uncertain; an attempt, perhaps, to take on board changing values, to explore and even exploit them, and finally to project an Ealing version of Britain in transition which would show the future as developing gradually from the past.[104]*

Mandy is a family melodrama and Mackendrick's only non-comedy at Ealing. It examines issues arising around post-war political and social changes. The defeat of the Socialist government by the Conservatives had reinvigorated debate abound the Welfare State, social responsibility and national values. The family should take responsibility, not the community; the individual should stand on their own feet and look after themselves, not expect the State to do it. Philip Kemp reminds us of the film's context, made a few weeks after the Conservative victory:

> *To such people the Tory victory of 1951 had come as an inexpressible relief. Mackendrick's film ... reflects that moment of transition. Christine.... embodies all the left-liberal, welfare state values that her husband's family mistrust and fear.*[105]

Mandy is both an examination of a 'social problem' with the spectator placed as objective observer, and also a melodrama appealing to its audience through its subjective depiction of personal human emotions. The social problem is focused around the education and integration of children who have special needs. Its serious subject required a partly documentary style using scenes filmed at the Royal Residential School for the Deaf at Clyne House in Old Trafford, Manchester. With only a few exceptions, the pupils from that school played the deaf children in the film. The most notable of the exceptions was Mandy herself, eight-year-old Mandy Miller who had had a small part in *The Man in the White Suit*. Her natural ability was brilliantly directed by Mackendrick who, along with the sound editor Stephen Dalby, created the experience of deafness, devising a technique of 'subjective non-sound'. He termed this as 'the silence of holding one's breath'.

The source material for Nigel Balchin's screenplay was a novel *The Day is Ours* by Hilda Lewis. It had been serialised on the BBC Radio Home Service (the equivalent to Radio 4) in *Woman's Hour*. Although very little of the original novel was maintained this was a subject that specifically targeted a female middle class audience, and was promoted by the Studio as a compelling family drama. The film begins by using some of the devices of the melodrama – the 'woman's picture' – opening with a female voice over. The voice is that of Christine Garland (she will be addressed sometimes as 'Chris' or 'Kit') and she describes herself as 'Just an ordinary housewife'. It is a mother's point of view, and it is a mother who primarily motivates the narrative conflict through her decisions and her actions.

Trapped in her grandparents barren garden

The initial conflict is between Christine and her husband Harry and their sharply diverging ideas on how to cope with their deaf daughter Mandy. They are a couple who appear to be living a relaxed, loving and normal life in a small, comfortable home but the discovery of Mandy's deafness begins the rift in their relationship. Harry's response to his daughter's affliction is to move his family back to live with his parents in their large formal house where Mandy's life becomes regulated by her grandmother and her governess. Harry's father takes no part in domestic affairs; his contact with the outside world is through playing chess by post. Mandy is isolated as she rides her tricycle round and round the barren garden. Her attempts to enter the world which she can see through the gate end in panic, frustration and mutual misunderstanding.

Christine needs to take control and to assert herself in the face of Harry's parents' conservative attitudes and Harry's own opposition. She sees that Mandy needs to be taken out of the stifling confines of the house so that she can learn to communicate with what surrounds it. Her conflict with Harry escalates until he strikes her, which fuels her decision to take Mandy away and breaks her dependence on the oppressive family. Later Harry is told by his solicitor 'striking a woman is always a mistake' not because it is the wrong thing to do, but because it gives her justification for removing herself and her child.

Christine experiences initial misgivings about sending Mandy to the special school which appears forbidding and alien, but she is encouraged to do so by her friends Lily and Jimmy whose family life is such a contrast to her own. Easy going, messy and artistic, they personify the 'new Bohemians' with their 'new left liberal welfare state values'. What first appeared as a forbidding Gothic institution run by an irritable and abrupt headmaster is later suggested as a family structure where Jane Ellis is the wise grandmother figure and Dick Searle (played by Jack Hawkins, the 'new face of Ealing') is the father offering an alternative to the rigid outlook of the Garland home, more outward looking and inclusive. This brings them into conflict with another example of the old guard, the school's governing body whose chairman Ackland is the personification of Tory suspicions about state education. The governors are mistrustful of Searle's methods and Ackland in particular is looking for ways to discredit him.

The film shifts its emphasis and branches out into a second female conflict: Mandy struggles to literally find *her* voice as she has to learn to speak and communicate, to battle with the

Social problem meets melodrama, Mandy says her first word

everyday world which she finds so difficult to enter. She can't adapt to institutional life, she needs to be with her mother. Christine becomes a single independent woman, living with her daughter in a comparatively shabby flat, free from the dead hand of her in-laws and in control of her own life. She is teetering on the brink of romance with Dick Searle (although she denies it) but her sexual needs have to be sublimated to her 'natural' function as mother, essential to the well being and development of her child. In a key sequence of the film the social problem and the emotional conflict of the maternal melodrama are seen to dovetail together. Mandy is seen at school with her teacher Miss Stockton learning to articulate different sounds. We then cut to Searle coaching Mandy in her flat whilst Christine prepares dinner. Mandy struggles and then articulates her first spoken word 'Mummy'. Christine's reaction to this breakthrough is to throw her arms around Searle and kiss him, an action observed by her downstairs neighbour who has been asked to report any such contact. The objective look at how a deaf child battles to speak has been merged into a subjective narrative of a woman's emotional response. News of Christine's reaction brings her husband back to control her. The opportunity to exist outside of her

113

marriage is curtailed. Mandy's breakthrough is not apparent as Christine has to take her back to the home of her in-laws, rejoining the family she briefly escaped and a jealous husband who refuses to see things from her point of view. Harry has surrendered his own freedom, resorting to dependence on his parents; Christine and Mandy will have to give up theirs.

The conclusion is a compromise. Mandy's grandfather hears her speak for the first time and takes charge. Harry has vacillated throughout the film, unable to overcome the obstacles of his daughter's deafness or his wife's separation. He is ordered by his father to assume responsibility: it is not her mother who can release Mandy but her father. Mandy leaves the house and the garden and goes to a group of ordinary children who play in the space outside. She is able to tell them her name and is invited to join in with them. She has been set free from the old world that stifled her. Pam Cook argues that the film presents a set of contradictions:

> *that in negotiating sets of competing and conflicting ideologies it produces a vision of Britain that is at once forward and backward looking – looking forward, that is, to a new egalitarian society in which boundaries of class and sex are broken down, and looking backward to traditional structures in order to preserve them.* Mandy *projects a picture of a nation on the brink of change, from which it ultimately draws back, sadly unable to rise to the challenge. Ealing itself was in the same position.*[106]

The 'competing and conflicting ideologies' have posited alternatives through the experiences of Mandy and Christine. The institution was impersonal; life was not easy for a single mother. Mandy is reabsorbed into the traditional family structure, from which she can now negotiate the outside world. Christine makes a move to follow her into that world but is prevented from doing so by Harry. She began the film with a voice over; at the end it is Mandy who speaks and Christine who watches in silence as Harry holds her back.

The Cruel Sea

This is a story of the Battle of the Atlantic, the story of an ocean, two ships and a handful of men. The men are the heroes, the heroines are the ships, the only villain is the sea, the cruel sea that man has made more cruel.
Jack Hawkins' opening voice-over, *The Cruel Sea*

The representation of women was never a priority at Ealing. Many accounts of the Studio stress it as a male province – Douglas Slocombe described it as a club; Michael Relph remarked on its public school ethos. By the 1950s however traditional images of masculinity were shifting. Men were faced with the task of living up to gender expectations when their roles as breadwinners and valiant and virile decision makers were being eroded. Harry's father had had to step in to make Harry see that he needed to be more decisive in his actions. The wartime image of British masculinity was that of bravery, resilience and stoicism. In a time of changing values it was necessary to remind the public of such values.

Balcon had talked in 1945 of presenting the world with

a complete picture of Britain....Britain as a leader in Social reform in the defeat of social injustice and a champion of civil liberties; Britain as a patron and parent of great writing, painting and music; Britain as a questing explorer, adventurer and trader; Britain as the home of great industry and craftsmanship; Britain as a mighty military power standing alone and undaunted against terrifying aggression.[107]

The Cruel Sea was one of Balcon's favourite films because he believed it to be the essence of 'undaunted Britishness'. Released in 1953 it was directed by Charles Frend who had also directed another of Balcon's favourites *Scott of the Antarctic* in 1948 with its image of the 'questing explorer'. Both films are prestige pictures that examine British heroics as an entirely male province. *Scott* was the kind of Technicolor spectacle that Rank was urging Balcon to make to attract the American market; an epic film about Robert Falcon Scott's ill-fated expedition to the South Pole in 1910–12. Filmed largely on location in Norway with a score by Ralph Vaughan Williams that later became part of his *Sinfonia Antarctica* it was chosen for the Royal Command Performance. It received wide acclaim with newspapers such as the *Sunday Dispatch* using their review of the film to revive what they saw as flagging patriotism:

> *Such a film as* Scott *is welcome at a time when other races speak disparagingly of our 'crumbling Empire' and our 'lack of spirit'. It should make those who have listened too closely to such talk believe afresh that ours is the finest breed of men on this earth. And so it is.*[108]

Scott begins, as does *The Cruel Sea*, with an image of the sea, stressing that we are an island race with a tradition as explorers. Scott's voice over links him and others like him with such a tradition 'other explorers before me'. There is a hint of ownership and indisputable right – 'I think an Englishman should get there first.' This determination to be first at the Pole leads him to make mistakes that end in failure. The film then is not about winning but taking part. Heroism is exactly that – the province of heroes not heroines. Women passively accept the decisions made by men and then patiently wait for them to carry them out.

Five years after *Scott* they are still waiting. *The Cruel Sea*, adapted from the book written in 1951 by Nicholas Montserrat and scripted by Eric Ambler, was a big commercial success. It forms part of the reconstruction of a war that was now passing into myth. The nostalgia for Britain's 'finest hour' had been invoked by Churchill as a Conservative promise. The Coronation of Elizabeth II in 1953 was seen as heralding a new Elizabethan era that would reassert the place Britain had occupied in the world in the 16th century: the days of Francis Drake and the Spanish Armada. The concept of Britain as one nation able to diffuse differences in order to fight a common enemy was no longer the necessity it had been. Now it was middle class white men who were seen to have fought the War for Britain, officers set apart from the other ranks by their courage and determination. Most of the film takes place at sea on board the corvette *Compass Rose* and later the frigate *Saltash Castle*. The real enemy that they face is the sea and the Germans, unseen in their U boats and only appearing at the end of the film, are part of this force of nature.

The structure of the ships echoes the structure of British society with Captain Ericson and his officers giving orders above and the ordinary seamen carrying them out below. The officers, distinguished by their received pronunciation, are drafted from civilian life, with previous middle class occupations such as journalist and barrister. The obnoxious Second in Command Bennett emphasises his position as a 'stickler for rules' but he is not a natural leader having been a used car salesman. He is soon dispatched and Lockhart, more secure in his middle class position, takes his place.

There are of course no women on board and their role in the conflict is at best peripheral. In 1942 the women of Bramley End had played their part and become assassins; by 1953 their roles have changed. They exist to provide a link with the normality of civilian life – the homely sister who dies in an air raid, the loving wife who waits and her opposite number, the vain unfaithful wife who betrays and humiliates her man. Julie, the blonde well bred Servicewoman who provides the rather tepid love interest for Lockhart acknowledges the close bond that exists between him and Captain Ericson with the observation 'women don't often have that relationship and if they do it's not usually about something important like running a ship or fighting a war'. Women know their place in the emotional pecking order. Heterosexual relationships are unsatisfactory as the real relationships are those between men in crisis situations. On board ship male bonding is essential, and is 'about the only one the war allows you'. The community and family are that of men, just as it was in Paddington Green Police station in *The Blue Lamp*.

"No one murdered them. It's the War. The whole bloody War"

The Cruel Sea tests its characters and puts its leading men under stress. Whilst we can see it as an examination of masculine values it is also a film in which it is the central male character who is the one allowed to express emotion. The key sequence is the one where Captain Ericson (played by Jack Hawkins) suspects that a U boat is tracking the fleet and its suspected position is immediately below a group of British sailors in the water waiting to be rescued. Ericson has to make the impossible choice of launching depth charges and thus sacrificing those few seamen in order to prevent the U Boat inflicting more casualties. His action is met with disbelief and even a cry of 'bloody murderer!' from one of his crew, and in fact his supposition is not proved as there is no final evidence of the U Boat's existence. He takes refuge in getting drunk, highly disturbed by what he has done, what he has been forced to do. In playing the scene Jack Hawkins cried. Balcon was very uneasy – a sailor and a captain would never cry, the image of men in the British War film had been that of stoicism and restraint. Balcon asked for the scene to be reshot with no tears, and then for another reshoot with just a hint of tears. In the end he agreed to the original take, admitting that Hawkins was right. In a moral dilemma decisive and unemotional action is needed as is learning 'how to die without wasting anyone's time', but subsequent emotion is not weakness. Ericson talks later in the film of war's 'dehumanising' effect, but in fact some post-war films allowed individual human emotions of sadness, fear, weariness and regret: 'No one murdered them. It's the war. The whole bloody war.'

Ealing at war. This is where we came in.

100 The 1951 Festival of Britain presented a picture of Britain to the world described by Michael Frayn as: 'the Britain of the radical middle classes – the do-gooders; the readers of the *News Chronicle*, *The Guardian* and *The Observer*; the signers of petitions; the backbone of the BBC.'

101 Pam Cook (1986) '*Mandy*, Daughter of Transition', in Barr, *All Our Yesterdays*, *op. cit.*, p. 355.

102 Philip Kemp, *Lethal Innocence*, *op. cit.*, p. 83.

103 This was the boom that would initiate Harold Macmillan's famous remark in 1957: 'Most of our people have never had it so good.' The Home Secretary R. A. Butler was to say in 1960: 'We have developed an affluent, open and democratic society... in which people are divided not so much between "haves" and "have-nots" as between "haves" and "have-mores".'

104 Pam Cook in Barr, *All Our Yesterdays*, *op. cit.*, p. 356.

105 Philip Kemp, *Lethal Innocence*, *op. cit.*, p. 77.

106 Pam Cook in Barr, *All Our Yesterdays*, *op. cit.*, p. 358.

107 Balcon (1945) as quoted in Barr, *Ealing Studios*, *op. cit.*, p. 60.

108 1948 review in the *Sunday Dispatch* quoted in Barr, *Ealing Studios*, *op. cit.*, p. 77.

10. EALING STUDIOS: THE END OF THE LINE

*Evaporation was a natural thing. We at Ealing knew
that the days were over before the public did. I do think
that movies, popular cinema entertainment, are not
monumental things for the ages – they belong to their
periods and should not last longer than their periods.*

Alexander Mackendrick[109]

Life was indeed changing for the British film industry. Film
audiences, so buoyant in the immediate post-war years, were
declining just as the costs of production were accelerating.
In a pamphlet published in 1951 by the Film Industry
Employees' Council (FIEC) the numbers of people employed
by feature film production companies (all staff that were
not artists or musicians) were given as having fallen from
7,739 in December 1948 to 3,340 in February 1951. The FIEC
blamed the crisis on two connected factors: the monopoly
of the industry by the two 'Oriental Potentates' and unfair
competition with Hollywood films. Between them Rank's
Odeon/Gaumont-British and John Maxwell's Associated
British Picture Corporation owned 70% of the large cinemas in
city centres. They had first pick of the films and could charge
higher ticket prices. They were thus able to decide 'which
films will cover costs and which will not. They can virtually
dictate which films the public shall or shall not see.' The FIEC
asked for 'bargaining power based on the quality of our films'
as the popularity of Hollywood films led to them being given
preference over our home grown product:

*Britain has long been Hollywood's largest and most
profitable market. Every American film – good, bad and
indifferent – has been certain of profitable showing here...*

we ask that conditions of fair competition be created.

The actor Sir Laurence Olivier added his voice:

It must be remembered that the American film has paid for itself before being shown here. We are a nice wedge of cream on the top for them. We are delighted to let them have it, but we would like some milk.[110]

The industry, already seen as in crisis by 1951, was to come up against another adversary the following year when the BBC began the national transmission of TV. This was boosted in 1953 by the televising of the Coronation when 2,000,000 people had sets, and then in 1955 with the introduction of a second channel, the commercially funded ITV, with its more populist and less middle class oriented programming. People's lifestyles and leisure habits were changing and cinema was losing the place it had held as the prime provider of entertainment. Annual box office admissions which had peaked at 1,635 million in 1946 had fallen to 1,396 million by 1950 and 1182 million by 1955.[111] Cinemas began to close.

The Titfield Thunderbolt and the End of Ealing Studios

It was very male-orientated; and another thing I criticise Ealing for is the class stereotypes....The market changed and I don't think Balcon did. **Roy Gough**[112]

As the decade progressed the traditional values of Britishness as represented in the Ealing films became more and more isolated. American influenced popular culture was seized on by the young and the social change that would mark the following decade was pointing towards the future, not dwelling on the past. The nostalgic comedy *The Titfield Thunderbolt*

The Titfield Thunderbolt, a relic taken out of a museum

(1953), directed by Charles Crichton and written by T. E. B. Clarke, is a film whose values can be seen to encapsulate those of the Studio withdrawing into itself to create communities when such communities were becoming, like the train of the title, obsolete. Comparisons can be drawn with Clarke's other comedies such as *Passport to Pimlico*. In *Pimlico* post-war England debates how to rebuild itself by drawing on the spirit of the recent past, the reality of a bomb damaged London and the common frustrations caused by restriction. In *The Titfield Thunderbolt* a post Labour Britain escapes to the fantasy world of a small community whose dream is to run a railway. It is an idealised rural England of thatched cottages and leafy lanes; Douglas Slocombe used the Technicolor cinematography to create an unreal world where the trees, fields and houses look like painted sets from Toytown. The quaint romanticised village is a world frozen in nostalgia, where Thomas the Tank Engine and the Fat Controller are able to bring the story to the right conclusion and everyone is happy. A group of villagers are trying to prevent British Railways (now a nationalised industry) from closing the Titfield railway branch line. Volunteers led by the clergyman and the local squire (the church and the landed gentry have regained their rightful places as leaders of the community) take the decision to run the line themselves, funded by the local businessman who is persuaded to do so by the promise of a train bar that is open outside licensing hours, and helped by the bishop who is a train enthusiast. The 'Thunderbolt' steam train itself is obsolete, a relic taken out of a museum.[113]

Ealing's commitment to a certain kind of quaint British eccentricity was to contribute to its downfall. As Philip Kemp notes:

> ...fantasy shades off into whimsy, individuality into eccentricity. There are still enjoyable moments, but it's hard not to lose patience with the pervasive air of parochial self-indulgence as Ealing's vision turns increasingly in on itself.[114]

The writer of *Titfield* himself acknowledged that the Ealing vision had become blinkered and had run out of steam:

> The world was changing so much. This little close knit community had failed to see how life was changing around us.[115]

In 1952 Ealing's major shareholder, Steven Courtauld, who had supported the studios since the ATP period, resigned for health reasons and left England for Rhodesia. With his departure Ealing lost the backing he had secured from the National Provincial Bank. Rank increased their finance of the studio to 75 per cent.

Balcon negotiated a large loan from the National Film Finance Corporation (NFFC) but Ealing continued to struggle. The only way to pay off the loan was to sell the Studio, its greatest asset. In 1955 it was sold to the BBC for just over £300,000. The sale of the Studio buildings coincided with the release of *The Ladykillers*, which as we have seen can be read as an ironic comment on change.

Balcon had a plaque placed on the studio wall that read: 'Here, during a quarter of a century, many films were made projecting Britain and the British character.'

He was determined to keep the team together. His plan had been to move to Rank's studios at Pinewood but, although Ealing had been financed and distributed by them for eleven years, Rank was not prepared to let them have exclusive use of one of its stages. In 1956 Balcon negotiated with MGM to continue making films at their studios in Borehamwood. He re-established the studio, now renamed Ealing Films, announcing:

> There we shall go on making dramas with a documentary background and comedies about ordinary people with the stray eccentric amongst them – films about daydreamers, mild anarchists, little men who long to kick the boss in the teeth.[116]

He hoped that MGM would distribute the films in the USA but shortly after the move Arthur Loew, his friend and contact at MGM, left. Balcon once again found himself at odds with the Hollywood major and was unable to gain any terms. Without its backing and its home the Studio lost the coherence that had contributed to its success. After making six films in three years Ealing ceased production in 1957.

The Legacy of Ealing

The BBC expanded their production base from Shepherd's Bush by moving into Ealing in the same year their monopoly of TV broadcasting ended and they themselves had to modernise in the face of competition from ITV. The British film industry was antagonistic to its rival and exhibitors at first imposed an embargo on showing old films on television as TV appeared to be the enemy that was killing the film industry and taking over its territory. The enemy however was to provide different opportunities for their conquered subjects and the smaller studios such as Teddington and Bushey began to make productions for the small screen. By 1957 all studios except Pinewood and Shepperton were producing both television and feature films.

Ealing became the heart of BBC TV film production and as Charles Barr writes: 'Ealing were taken over by television but infiltrated its conqueror.'[117] One of the first series to be made there was *Dixon of Dock Green*, the spin off from *The Blue Lamp*. Written by Ted Willis and with Jack Warner reprising his original role it ran from 1955 to 1976. It was a reminder of a cosy community, and, as in the film, pictured life at Dock Green police station being like a family with Dixon himself the father. Each episode ended with him philosophising documentary style direct to camera on the evils of crime.

As a public service broadcaster the BBC had to maintain a strong sense of values. Funded by licence fee they did not have to make money; they could do work that they found interesting. The tradition of realism and the emphasis on writing and performance, so fundamental to Ealing, were carried on. Television has provided the training ground for directors, writer and performers who have subsequently made feature films. Some successful British films have carried on what has been seen as the Ealing spirit and the phrase 'like an Ealing Comedy' has been used frequently. Michael Brooke wrote of *A Private Function* (dir. Malcolm Mowbray, 1984 HandMade Films) that it:

> *may be the closest that 1980s British cinema came to recapturing the spirit of the great Ealing comedies. There may be more emphasis on sex and lower bodily functions,*

> *but it's still a perfect double-bill partner for* Passport to Pimlico.[118]

When Charles Crichton directed *A Fish Called Wanda* in 1988 its parentage was suggested in reviews such as:

> *Veteran director Charles Crichton and scriptwriter-star John Cleese create a dazzling quilt from various strands of English and American comedy. The plot, in which four disparate characters attempt a daring heist, comes from Ealing caper comedies, such as Crichton's own* The Lavender Hill Mob.... *The movie pays savage tribute to another Ealing comedy,* The Ladykillers, *as Palin attempts to kill a witness to the gang's getaway.*[119]

Both *Brassed Off* (dir. Mark Herman, 1996 Channel 4 Films) and *The Full Monty* (dir. Peter Cattaneo, 1997 Redwave Films/Channel 4 Films) were seen as continuing the themes of community and emphasis on screenplay and performance so prominent in Ealing films. Reviewing *Brassed Off* the Radio Times saw:

> *a certain Ealing-like quality in the way the mining town of Grimley rallies around the colliery's brass band as it progresses to the national finals amid talk of pit closures and redundancies.*

Both of these films deal with specific British regional working class communities under stress in difficult times but exhibiting resilience, humour and the camaraderie that enable them to deal with such circumstances. The notion of the collective, underlined by performing together, allows the group to triumph. *The Full Monty* was a big international success without compromising its British flavour and subject matter. Julia Hallam observed:

The nostalgic construction of working class values is a reminder of the kind of British films that were popular at the box office when the UK had a more robust film industry. A hankering for the spirit of Ealing ghosts both these bittersweet comedies, the Ealing of that brief post-war period when a focus on whimsical characters in small communities pulling together for the common good projected an idealised version of a nation united by adversity.[120]

In 1980 David Puttnam dedicated his patriotic Oscar winning *Chariots of Fire* (dir. Hugh Hudson, Enigma Productions) to Michael Balcon: '*Chariots* was for and to an extent about Michael Balcon. I like to think *Chariots* was a film of which Mick would have thoroughly approved.'[121]

The Studio that often looked back so fondly to the traditions of the past has now itself become the subject of nostalgia, continuing to be evoked as the embodiment of a particular notion of a Britain that no longer exists.[122]

Postscript

Since 1991 the fortunes of the Studio on Ealing Green with its landmark White Lodge have fluctuated. The buildings eventually became too expensive for the BBC to maintain and were purchased by the National Film & Television School (NFTS) in 1995 for £2.6 million, the intention being to move the school from its location in Beaconsfield outside London to a more central site. Soon after the purchase it was realised that the site and studios would cost too much to convert into a film school, and the project was abandoned.

In 1999 the *Ealing and Acton Gazette* carried the headline '*Ealing Studios Future in Doubt*'. The accompanying article stated:

> Fears are growing that Ealing Studios may be sold for business, retail, or housing development, ending film making at the site since the 1920s. ...Ealing Studios were let out to independent production companies but now the NFTS has decided to sell and the studios are again on the market with a question mark hanging over their future. Fuller Peiser, the NFTS planning consultants consider that the studios will not be easy to sell as studios to film and TV companies and can't rule out the possibilities of other uses.
>
> The area is earmarked by Ealing Council's Unity Development Plan for local employment and light industrial use. A council spokeswoman said the Planning Office had been told that the site would be marketed as a film studio and that the Council was keen to see Ealing's history of film and TV production continue.
>
> Ealing Studios is also included in the Ealing Green Conservation Area. The art deco White House building that fronts the site is considered to be of architectural importance although neither it nor the studio is listed. An Ealing Green resident considers that the vendors are looking for get-outs to obtain maximum revenue for the site as real estate, and says that Ealing Green residents would like to see the site continue as film or TV studios.
>
> However, there must be many covetous eyes of greedy developers eager to get their hands on this highly desirable site for development other than film and TV studios. Money and time will tell.[123]

Luckily the 'greedy developers' were kept at bay and in 2000 Barnaby Thompson led a consortium that bought the studios and invested millions in modernising the sound stages and production facilities to turn out theatrical films again. The BBC *Money Programme* entitled 'Once More with Ealing', broadcast in July 2007, looked forward to the release of *St Trinian's* (dirs. Oliver Parker, Barnaby Thompson) to 'recreate Ealing's golden days'.[124] In 2008 *Screen International* was able to report:

> *The West London-based Ealing Studios has completed the first two of three phases in a state-of-the-art regeneration, including renovations of production offices and dressing rooms, plus the construction of five new buildings.[James] Spring [managing director at Ealing Studios] hopes the campus's combination of studio space, high-tech offices and a green, relatively central location near a tube stop will make Ealing Studios an even more attractive destination for creative companies, including film-makers and small production outfits. Directors Oliver Parker and Gurinder Chadha and producers including Steve Clark-Hall are already based at Ealing. 'We want to give more of an opportunity for writers and directors to have a home here, to build that Ealing community,' Spring says. 'People like the idea of a community that creates business opportunities and creative opportunities. And people just like being around other like-minded people.'[125]*

A hundred years after Will Barker set up his glass studio Ealing continues to make the news. In the last thirty-five years the Studio has been the subject of major studies – by John Ellis in 1975, Charles Barr in 1977 and George Perry in 1981 – all of which have been invaluable in the writing of this book. There have been TV programmes, Film Festivals and numerous articles, analyses, reviews and tributes. It seems fitting however to let Michael Balcon have the last word, his comment on the publication of Barr's book in 1977:

A great many motives were attributed to why we made the films we did; all I can say is that we just enjoyed making films.

109   Alexander Mackendrick (1986) interview *Omnibus: Made in Ealing*, *op. cit.*

110   *The Crisis of British Films*, pamphlet published by the Film Industry Employees' Council, March 1951, p. 9.

111   Of course there was much worse to come. By 1960 the figure had fallen to 515 million and by 1971 to 146 million.

112   Roy Gough, still photographer at Ealing, interviewed by Robin Buss, 'England's Dreaming', *op. cit.* [Query:page number?]

113   Steam trains were becoming obsolete but many branch lines were to follow suit. Ten years after the film was made The Beeching Report, *The Re-shaping of British Railways*, resulted in their closure.

114   Philip Kemp @ http://www.filmreference.com/Writers-and-Production-Artists-Ch-De/ Clarke-T-E-B.html , *op. cit.*

115   T. E. B Clarke in an interview (1986) *Omnibus: Made in Ealing*, *op. cit.*

116   Balcon in 1956 as quoted in Barr, *Ealing Studios*, *op. cit.*

117   Charles Barr, *Ealing Studios*, *op. cit.*, p. 180.

118   http://www.screenonline.org.uk/film/id/452437/.

119   http://uk.rottentomatoes.com/m/fish_called_wanda/.

120   Julia Hallam (2000) 'Film, Class and National Identity: Re-imagining Communities in the Age of Devolution', in Ashby and Higson (eds) *British Cinema Past and Present*, London: Routledge, p. 267.

121   David Puttnam, Preface to *Michael Balcon: The Pursuit of British Cinema*, *op. cit.*, p. 18.

122   Although it no longer exists attempts are made to revive it. At the Barbican 'Best Ever' Ealing Film Season, 1st–26th August 1993, the programme carried the addition: 'To complement this programme of English films traditional cream teas are available in the Waterside Restaurant.'

123   Bob Allen based on a report in the *Ealing & Acton Gazette*, 9 March 1999.

124   *The Money Programme: Once More with Ealing* BBC 2, 27 July 2007. Some success had been achieved with *The Importance of Being Earnest* (Oliver Parker, 2002) and *Valiant* (Gary Chapman, 2005)

125   Wendy Mitchell, 'In Focus: the Ealing Studios Revamp', *Screen International*, 12 September 2008.

EALING STUDIOS SELECTED FILMOGRAPHY

List of films mentioned in the text. For a complete list of Ealing Studio Films see Barr, *Ealing Studios*.

Convoy Penrose Tennyson, 1940.

Associate Producer: Sergei Nalbandov; Screenplay: Penrose Tennyson, Patrick Kirwan; Cinematography: Wilkie Cooper, Gordon Dines; Editor: Ray Pitt; Art Director: Wilfred Shingleton; Music: Ernest Irving.

Clive Brook (Captain Armitage), John Clements (Lieut. Cranford), Judy Campbell (Lucy Armitage).

The Foreman Went to France aka *Somewhere in France* Charles Frend, 1942.

Associate Producer: Alberto Cavalcanti; Screenplay: John Dighton, Angus MacPhail, Leslie Arliss based by J. B. Priestley on the true story of Melbourne Johns; Cinematography: Wilkie Cooper; Editor: Robert Hamer; Art Director: Tom Morahan; Music: William Walton.

Tommy Trinder (Tommy Hoskins), Gordon Jackson (Jock Macfarlane), Constance Cummings (Anne Stafford), Clifford Evans (Fred Carrick), Robert Morley (French Mayor).

Went the Day Well? aka *48 Hours* Alberto Cavalcanti, 1942.

Producer: Michael Balcon; Screenplay: Angus MacPhail, John Dighton and Diana Morgan from a story by Graham Green; Cinematography: Wilkie Cooper, Douglas Slocombe; Editor: Sidney Cole; Art Director: Tom Morahan; Music: William Walton.

Leslie Banks (Oliver Wilsford), Valerie Taylor (Nora Ashton), Basil Sydney (Kommandant Orlter, alias Major Hammond), Harry Fowler (George Truscott), Edward Rigby (Bill Purvis), Marie Lohr (Mrs Frazer), C. V. France (Vicar), Mervyn Johns (Sims), Muriel George (Mrs Collins).

San Demetrio, London Charles Frend, 1943.

Associate producer: Robert Hamer; Screenplay: Robert Hamer, Charles Frend from the factual narrative by F. Tennyson Jesse;

Cinematography: Ernest Palmer; Art Director: Duncan Sutherland; Music :John Greenwood.

Walter Fitzgerald (Chief Engineer Pollard), Ralph Michael (Second Officer Hawkins), Frederick Piper (Bosun Fletcher), Gordon Jackson (Jamieson), Mervyn Johns (Boyle), Robert Beatty ("Yank" Preston)

Dead of Night Alberto Cavalcanti (*Christmas Story, Ventriloquist's Dummy*), Robert Hamer (*Haunted Mirror*), Charles Crichton (*Golfing Story*), Basil Dearden (*Linking Story, Hearse Driver*), 1945.

Producers: Sidney Cole, John Croydon; Screenplay: John Baines, Angus MacPhail; Additional Dialogue: T. E. B. Clarke; Cinematography: Stan Pavey, Douglas Slocombe; Editor: Charles Hasse; Art Director: Michael Relph; Music: Georges Auric.

Mervyn Johns (Walter Craig), Frederick Valk (Dr Van Straaten), Anthony Baird (Hugh), Sally Ann Howes (Sally O'Hara), Googie Withers (Joan Cortland), Ralph Michael (Peter Cortland), Basil Radford (George Parratt), Naunton Wayne (Larry Potter), Michael Redgrave (Maxwell Frere), Harley Power (Sylvester Kee).

Hue and Cry Charles Crichton, 1947.

Associate Producer: Henry Cornelius; Screenplay: T. E. B. Clarke; Cinematography: Douglas Slocombe; Editor: Charles Hasse; Art Director: Norman G. Arnold; Music: Georges Auric.

Harry Fowler (Joe Kirby), Jack Warner (Nightingale), Alastair Sim (Felix H. Wilkinson), Joan Dowling (Clarry), Douglas Barr (Alec).

It Always Rains on Sunday Robert Hamer, 1947.

Associate Producer: Henry Cornelius; Screenplay: Angus MacPhail, Robert Hamer, and Henry Cornelius based on the novel by Arthur le Bern; Cinematography: Douglas Slocombe; Editor: Michael Truman; Art Director: Duncan Sutherland; Music: Georges Auric.

Googie Withers (Rose Sandigate), Edward Chapman (George Sandigate), John McCallum (Tommy Swann), Jack Warner (Det. Sgt. Fothergill), Susan Shaw (Vi Sandigate), Sidney Taffler (Morris Hyams), John Slater (Lou Hyams), Meier Tzelnicker (Solly Hyams).

Saraband for Dead Lovers Basil Dearden, 1948.

Associate Producer: Michael Relph; Screenplay: John Dighton, Alexander Mackendrick from the novel by Helen Simpson; Technicolor Cinematography: Douglas Slocombe; Editor: Michael Truman; Art Director: Michael Relph, Jim Morahan, William Kellner; Music: Alan Rawsthorne.

Stewart Grainger (Konigsmark), Joan Greenwood (Sophie Dorothea), Flora Robson (Countess Platen).

Scott of the Antarctic Charles Frend, 1948.

Associate Producer: Sidney Cole; Screenplay: Ivor Montagu, Walter Meade, Mary Haley Bell; Technicolor Cinematography: Jack Cardiff, Osmond Borradaile, Geoffrey Unsworth; Editor: Peter Tanner; Art Director: Arne Akermark; Music: Ralph Vaughan Williams later reworked into his Sinfonia Antarctica.

John Mills (Capt. Scott), Derek Bond (Capt. Oates), Harold Warrender (Dr Wilson), James Robertson Justice (PO Taff Evans), Reginald Beckwith (Lieut. Bowers), Kenneth More (Lieut. Teddy Evans).

Passport to Pimlico Henry Cornelius, 1949.

Associate Producer: E. V. H. Emmett; Screenplay: T. E. B. Clarke; Cinematography: Lionel Banes; Editor: Michael Truman; Art Director: Roy Oxley; Music: Georges Auric.

Stanley Holloway (Arthur Pemberton), John Slater (Frank Huggins), Raymond Huntley (Mr W. P. J. Wix), Margaret Rutherford (Professor Hatton-Jones), Barbara Murray (Shirley Pemberton).

Whisky Galore! aka *Tight Little Island* Alexander Mackendrick, 1949.

Associate Producer: Monja Danischewsky; Screenplay: Angus MacPhail, Compton Mackenzie adapted from his novel; Cinematography: Gerald Gibbs; Editor and Music: Ernest Irving.

Basil Radford (Captain Paul Waggett), Bruce Seton (Sergeant Odd), John Gregson (Sammy MacCodrun), Gordon Jackson (George Campbell), Joan Greenwood (Peggy Macroon).

Kind Hearts and Coronets Robert Hamer, 1949.

Associate Producer: Michael Relph; Screenplay: Robert Hamer, John Dighton from the novel *Israel Rank* by Roy Horniman; Cinematography: Douglas Slocombe, Jeff Seaholme; Editor: Peter Tanner; Art Director: William Kellner, Music: Ernest Irving and Mozart, *Don Giovanni.*

Dennis Price (Louis Mazzini), Alec Guinness (Ethelred Duke of Chalfont, Lord Ascoyne d'Ascoyne, the Reverend Henry d'Ascoyne, General Lord Rufus d'Ascoyne, Admiral Lord Horatio d'Ascoyne, Ascoyne d'Ascoyne, Henry d'Ascoyne, Lady Agatha d'Ascoyne), Valerie Hobson (Edith D'Ascoyne), Joan Greenwood (Sibella Holland).

The Blue Lamp Basil Dearden, 1950.

Producer: Michael Relph; 2nd Unit Direction: Alexander Mackendrick; Screenplay: T. E. B. Clarke from a story by Ted Willis and Jan Read, additional dialogue Alexander Mackendrick; Cinematography: Gordon Dines; Editor: Peter Tanner; Art Director: Tom Morahan; Music: Ernest Irving.

Jack Warner (PC George Dixon), Jimmy Hanley (PC Andy Mitchell), Dirk Bogarde (Tom Riley), Peggy Evans (Diana Lewis), Bernard Lee (Divisional Detective Inspector Cherry), Gladys Henson (Mrs Dixon), Robert Flemyng (Sgt. Roberts).

Pool of London Basil Dearden, 1950.

Producer: Michael Balcon; Screenplay: Jack Whittingham, John Eldridge;   Cinematography: Gordon Dines; Editor: Peter Tanner; Art Director: Jim Morahan; Music: John Addison.

Michael Golden (Customs Official Andrews), Bonar Colleano (Dan MacDonald), Susan Shaw (Pat), Renee Asherson (Sally), Earl Cameron (Johnny).

The Lavender Hill Mob Charles Crichton, 1951.

Associate Producer: Michael Truman; Screenplay: T. E. B. Clarke; Cinematography: Douglas Slocombe; Editor: Seth Holt; Art Director: William Kellner; Music: George Auric.

Alec Guinness (Henry Holland), Stanley Holloway (Alfred Pendlebury),

Sidney James ('Lackery' Wood), Alfie Bass ('Shorty'), Marjorie Fielding (Mrs Chalk), Edie Martin (Miss Evesham).

The Man in the White Suit Alexander Mackendrick, 1951.

Associate Producer: Sidney Cole; Screenplay: John Dighton, Alexander Mackendrick Roger MacDougall from the play by Roger MacDougall; Cinematography: Douglas Slocombe; Editor: Bernard Gribble; Art Director: Jim Morahan; Music: Benjamin Frankel

Alec Guinness (Sidney Stratton), Joan Greenwood (Daphne Birnley),

Cecil Parker (Alan Birnley), Michael Gough (Michael Corland), Ernest Thesiger (Sir John Kierlaw).

Mandy aka *Crash of Silence* Alexander Mackendrick, 1952.

Producer: Leslie Norman; Screenplay: Nigel Balchin from the novel by Hilda Lewis; Cinematography: Douglas Slocombe; Editor: Seth Holt; Art Director: Jim Morahan; Music: William Alwyn.

Phyllis Calvert (Christine Garland), Jack Hawkins (Dick Searle), Terence Morgan (Harry Garland), Godfrey Tearle (Mr Garland), Mandy Miller (Mandy Garland), Nancy Price (Jane Ellis), Eleanor Summerfield (Lily Tabor), Edward Chapman (Ackland).

The Titfield Thunderbolt Charles Crichton, 1953.

Producer: Michael Truman; Screenplay: T. E. B. Clarke; Cinematography: Douglas Slocombe; Editor: Seth Holt; Art Director: C. P. Norman; Music: Georges Auric.

Stanley Holloway (Walter Valentine), George Relph (Vicar Sam Weech), John Gregson (Squire Gordon Chesterford), Hugh Griffith (Dan Taylor).

The Cruel Sea Charles Frend, 1953.

Producer: Leslie Norman; Screenplay: Eric Ambler from the novel by Nicholas Montserrat; Cinematography: Gordon Dines; Editor: Peter Tanner; Art Director: Jim Morahan; Music: Alan Rawsthorne.

Jack Hawkins (Lieut-Cdr.Ericson), Donald Sinden (Lieut. Lockhart), Denholm Elliott (Lieut. Morell), Stanley Baker (Bennett).

The Ladykillers Alexander Mackendrick, 1955.

Producer: Seth Holt; Screenplay: William Rose; Technicolor Cinematography: Otto Heller; Editor: Jack Harris; Art Director: Jim Morahan; Music: Tristram Cary.

Katie Johnson (Mrs Louisa Wilberforce), Alec Guinness (Professor Marcus), Peter Sellers (Harry), Cecil Parker (Major Courtney), Herbert Lom (Louis), Danny Green (One Round), Jack Warner (Police Superintendant).

BIBLIOGRAPHY

ALDGATE, Anthony and RICHARDS, Jeffrey (1986) *Britain Can Take It: The British Cinema in the Second World War*, Edinburgh: Edinburgh University Press

ASHBY, Justine and HIGSON, Andrew (eds) (2000) *British Cinema Past and Present*, London: Routledge

BALCON, Michael (1945) *The Producer: Lecture Given to the British Film Institute's Summer School on Film Appreciation*, London: BFI

BALCON, Michael (1969) *Michael Balcon Presents: A Lifetime of Films*, London: Hutchinson

BARR, Charles (1980) *Ealing Studios*, New York: Overlook Press

BARR, Charles (ed.) (1986) *All Our Yesterdays*, London: BFI

BROWN, Geoff and KARDISH, Laurence (1984) *Michael Balcon: The Pursuit of British Cinema*, New York: The Museum of Modern Art

CHAPMAN, James (2000) *The British at War: Cinema State and Propaganda 1939–1945*, London: I.B. Taurus

CURRAN, James and PORTER, Vincent (eds) (1983) *British Cinema History*, London: Weidenfeld and Nicholson

DANISCHEWSKY, Monja (ed.) (1947) *Michael Balcon's Twenty-Five Years in Film*, London: World Film Publications

ELLIS, John (1975) 'Made in Ealing', *Screen* (16) 1: Spring.

ELLIS, John (1978) 'The Discourse of Art Cinema', *Screen* (19) 3: Autumn.

GERAGHTY, Christine (2000) *British Cinema in the 1950s: Gender, Genre and the New Look*, London: Routledge

HILL, John (1986) *Sex, Class and Realism: British Cinema 1956–1963*, London: BFI

HURD, Geoff (ed.) (1984) *National Fictions: World War II in British Films and TV*, London: BFI

LEARY, Emmeline (1989) *Action! Comedy! Romance! Classic Film Posters from Ealing Studios*, Ealing Films Festival

KEMP, Philip (1991) *Lethal Innocence: The Cinema of Alexander Mackendrick*, London: Methuen

MURPHY, Robert (ed.) (2001) *The British Cinema Book*, London: BFI

PERRY, George (1981) *Forever Ealing*, London: Pavilion Books

PIRIE, David (2008) *A New Heritage of Horror: The English Gothic Cinema*, London: I.B. Taurus

RICHARDS, Jeffrey and ALDGATE, Anthony (2009) *Best of British: Cinema and Society 1930–1970*, London: I.B. Taurus

RICHARDS, Jeffrey (1977) *Films and British National Identity: From Dickens to Dad's Army*, Manchester: Manchester University Press

RICHARDS, Jeffrey (ed.) (1998) *The Unknown 30s: An Alternative History of the British Cinema 1929–1939*, London: I.B. Taurus

STREET, Sarah (1997) *British National Cinema*, London and New York: Routledge

Television Programmes

Omnibus: 'Made in Ealing: the Story of Ealing Studios', directed by Roland Keating BBC, 2 May 1986.

Forever Ealing, directed by Andrew Snell, Silver Apples Media in association with Studio Canal and Channel 4, Channel 4, 2002.

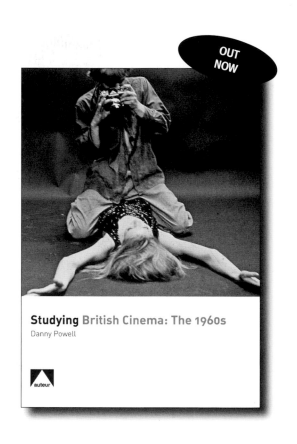

OUT NOW

Studying British Cinema: The 1960s

Danny Powell

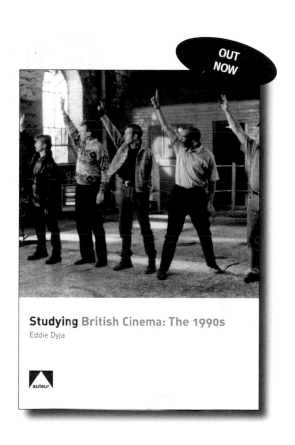

OUT NOW

Studying British Cinema: The 1990s

Eddie Dyja

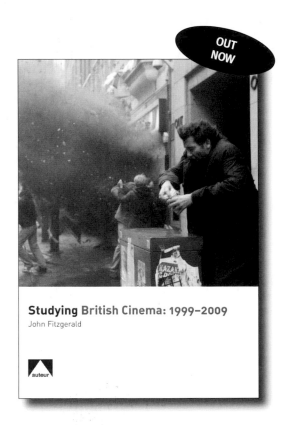

OUT NOW

Studying British Cinema: 1999–2009

John Fitzgerald